BLACKSMITHING

SkipJack Press
An Imprint of Finney Company

Notice to the Reader:
The information and material in this book, to the best of our knowledge, were accurate and true at the time of writing. All recommendations are made without guarantee on the part of the publisher. The publisher disclaims any liability in connection with the use of information contained in this book or the application of such information.

The reader is expressly warned to consider and adopt all safety precautions regarding blacksmithing and to avoid all potential hazards. By following the instructions herein, the reader willingly assumes all risks in connection with such instructions.

All rights reserved. No part of this publication may be reproduced or transmitted in any form or by any means, electronic or mechanical, including photocopy, recording, or any information storage and retrieval system without the written permission of the publisher.

ISBN: 978-1-879535-32-9
SkipJack Press Edition © 2018

Original Copyright © 1925
The Manual Arts Press

SkipJack Press
An Imprint of Finney Company
www.finneyco.com • www.astragalpress.com

The Selvidge Series of Instruction Manuals

BLACKSMITHING
A Manual for Use in School and Shop

BY

R. W SELVIDGE
PROFESSOR OF INDUSTRIAL EDUCATION
UNIVERSITY OF MISSOURI

AND

J M. ALLTON
INSTRUCTOR IN FORGING
UNIVERSITY OF MISSOURI

THE MANUAL ARTS PRESS
PEORIA, ILLINOIS

Copyright, 1925
THE MANUAL ARTS PRESS
33 C 91

PREFACE

THIS book is designed for use as a text in school shops and farm shops, and for the blacksmith who is interested in extending his knowledge and increasing his skill. It is one of a series of trade manuals developed on the plan set forth in the book *How to Teach a Trade.**

The material is organized in such a manner as to give the utmost flexibility in teaching the subject, and it makes possible individual instruction without increasing the burdens of the teacher. It also provides for the progress of the individual pupil according to his ability and application.

It is obvious that the first step in teaching a trade is to determine exactly what you wish to teach. In order to determine this it is necessary to have a comprehensive analysis of the trade. Such an analysis is provided in this manual. It is based upon what one must be able to *do* in order to be proficient in the trade, and upon what one must *know.*

What one must be able to do involves the operations, or the manipulative skills, of the trade. What one must know consists of the topics of information with which the worker must be familiar in order to plan his jobs and carry on his work successfully

With this analysis as the basis, instructions are given telling exactly *how* to perform the operations. This is a distinctive feature of the book. The instructions are the result of a number of years of practical experience in a general blacksmith shop as well as a number of years of experience in teaching blacksmithing to many grades and types of boys. The material and methods have been thoroly tested in classes of farm boys and of engineering students. In every case the classes have made unusually rapid progress and have developed an increased confidence and self-reliance. The

*Robert W Selvidge, The Manual Arts Press.

simple language and abundant illustrations make the directions easily understood.

Based upon the result of extended tests with boys and men of various grades of advancement, suggestions are given for the use of the manual. These methods have been highly successful but other practices or modifications of these might give equally good results.

The instructions cover the operations involved in forging and welding iron and steel, hardening and tempering, general repair work, tire setting and horseshoeing. The directions tell, step by step, how to perform each operation.

In dealing with the information topics the essential facts are stated briefly and without discussion. These are separated from the operations in order that they may be presented when needed and without unduly interfering with the development of skill in the manipulative operations.

THE AUTHORS.

University of Missouri, 1925

BLACKSMITHING
Analysis of the Trade

INSTRUCTION UNITS

Unit Operations

1. Building and Maintaining Forge Fire................13
2. Holding Work................15
3. Heating Work................17
4. Measuring and Cutting Stock................18
5. Drawing Out Stock................21
6. Bending Round and Rectangular Stock................23
7. Bending Eyes................25
8. Twisting................27
9. Upsetting................28
10. Heading................30
11. Punching................33
12. Forming Punched Eye................35
13. Fullering................38
14. Swaging................39
15. Striking................41
16. Welding................42
17. Forging Tool Steel................52
18. Annealing Tool Steel................53
19. Hardening Tool Steel................54
20. Tempering Tool Steel................55
21. Working High Speed Steel................58
22. Case-Hardening................59
23. Drilling................60
24. Tapping................62
25. Cutting Threads................64
26. Bending Pipe................65
27. Riveting................67
28. Removing Broken Stud Bolt................69
29. Sawing with Hack-Saw................71
30. Soldering................73
31. Brazing................76
32. Babbitting and Scraping Bearings................77
33. Filing................80
34. How to Sharpen a Saw................82
35. Setting Wagon Tire................85
36. Setting Buggy Tire................90

Analysis of the Trade

37 Renewing Buggy and Wagon Tires....................................94
38. Renewing Wagon Felloes 97
39. Renewing Half Rims..99
40. Replacing Spokes...101
41. Painting Repaired Parts 103
42. Sharpening Plow Shares 105
43. Pointing a Plow..108
44. Examination of Horses' Feet Preparatory to Shoeing..........111
45. Removing Old Shoes...113
46. Preparing Hoof for Shoe,...................................114
47 Fitting Horse Shoes...116
48. Nailing on Shoe..118

Information Topics

1. Location of Shop Equipment...................................122
2. The Forge..124
3. The Anvil..126
4. The Forge Fire...128
5. Fuel Used for Forge Fire,..................................129
6. Blacksmith Tools 130
7 Iron and Steel..136
8. Effect of Heat on Steel 138
9. Welding..140
10. Fluxes..142
11. Tempering Tool Steel......................................143
12. Shapes and Sizes of Wrought Iron, Mild Steel, and Tool Steel 144
13. Case-Hardening 146
14. Taps and Dies 147
15. Expansion of Iron and Steel...............................148
16. Files 149
17 Emery Wheel Test for Determining Kinds of Materials........150

Standard Tables

1. Weights of Round and Square Iron and Steel Bars.............152
   Weights of Flat Iron.......................................152
2. Weights of Octagon Bars,...................................153
3. Wire Gage Standards in United States 154
4. Bolts and Cap Screws.......................................155
5. Stove Bolts..155
6. Common Steel Wire Nails 156
7. Diameter of Wood Screws 156

HOW TO USE THE MANUAL

THIS manual is not intended to dispense with instruction on the part of the teacher, but it does supply well organized material of instruction in a permanent form available to the student at all times. In most instances these instructions will be found adequate but no book can supply the inspiration that comes from the personal contact of teacher and pupil. Neither can written instructions supply an ideal with respect to workmanship, which is the first step in the development of skill. These fundamental things must come from some other source and some provision must be made for them. One important advantage of having the instruction material organized in this form is that it gives the teacher more time and opportunity for individual contact, and he must not neglect this opportunity. The ideals with respect to what constitutes good workmanship must be supplied by demonstrations and by examples.

When we analyze any job which we wish to use as the basis for instruction we find that there are one or more distinct divisions, or points, we wish to emphasize. These divisions we call units of instruction and when they deal with manipulative operations we call them unit operations. These unit operations are selected as units of instruction because they occur in practically the same form as parts of a great many jobs. Since all jobs are made up of one or more of these operations in various combinations the plan has been to prepare definite instructions for performing each operation. The operations are divided into definite instructional steps. These instructions are prepared with great care and accuracy and are, in a condensed form, just what the instructor would give orally

With such an arrangement we have definite written instructions for every operation, or instruction unit, in any job that may arise. All we have to do is analyze the job to find out what operations are involved and we have the instructions for each operation organized and at hand. This gives an almost unlimited flexibility without increasing the burdens of the teacher

We do not give a list of jobs but every teacher should have such a list—a list much larger than he would expect any student to do. The instructor should analyze each of these jobs carefully and list the operations involved. Such an analysis enables him to determine more accurately the doing difficulty involved in the job and to determine whether the job involves the operations in which he wishes to give instruction.

The first jobs should be very simple ones, and the teacher should never assign a job until he is sure it is within the capacity of the student; but when the job is once assigned, the student should be held to a strict performance of the task.

It often is desirable to have a student go thru a certain amount of practice on these operations before he undertakes a project or job involving several operations; however, there is no objection to a student's undertaking any job he is capable of handling in a satisfactory manner.

The student should be required to analyze and plan his job before he begins work on it. It may help to think of the operations as the different objectives as one progresses with the job.

In the task of the analysis of the job some individual assistance may be necessary, but care must be taken to develop self-reliance on the part of the student. It is well to remember that time is not wasted that is spent in preliminary study and planning of the job. The ability to look at a job and tell what operations are involved and determine the proper order of procedure in doing them is one in which students will take great pride. The development of the ability to analyze and plan a job is so important that it is well to give considerable time to it even when the jobs are not to be done by the students.

It should be remembered that the development of skill is one of the objects of this training and that skill is a thoroly established habit that can be developed only thru much practice. A student should never be regarded as proficient in an operation until he can do it with speed and confidence.

In order that the student may appreciate and understand the value of the printed instructions, it is well in the beginning to have some member of the class read the instructions for an operation while the instructor performs the operation, step by step as directed. Such demonstrations should be given frequently in order to give the student an ideal, with respect to skill, toward which to work. It is also well to have a student perform an operation before the class as another reads the instructions. This will establish confidence in the instructions and give the students a feeling that with the instructions they will be able to work out their jobs without assistance.

There should always be many examples of good workmanship in the shop. There should be simple things, such as the beginner must do, as well as intricate ornamental work. This is necessary in order that the boy may know what constitutes good workmanship in the field of his immediate problem.

Before a student begins a job he should read carefully all the directions for performing the operations with which he is not already familiar He should have clearly in mind each step in performing the operations. It is by no means necessary that he have his book open before him, but he should have it at hand for reference if any difficulty arises. The class should be called together frequently for the discussion of the questions given in connection with the instructions, matters of information, and the consideration of any difficulties that may have arisen and means of overcoming them.

If we lay aside our old pedagogical formalism and examine the problem of shop teaching as it actually exists we will find that there are several distinct phases of instruction. This is true whether the instruction is given in written or in oral form.

1. *There must be a clear and definite statement of the problem or job so that the learner will know exactly what is required.*

This means that all drawings, specifications or instructions necessary for the completion of the job should be given to the student. He should also have a definite notion of the standard of workmanship required.

In order that the instructor may be sure that every detail of the instructions are understood the student should explain the instructions to the instructor More failures result from a want of a thoro understanding of what is required than from all other causes combined. Be absolutely sure that every detail of the requirement is understood.

2. *The student should analyze the job for the operations involved.*

In order that the student may do this readily at the beginning he should be given a list of the Unit Operations of the trade and on this he should check the operations involved in the particular job. This is a further verification of step one and assures the teacher that the student knows what is to be done. A few well-directed questions will lead the student to discover any errors in his analysis. He should also enter on the sheet his estimate of the time required for the job and at the completion of the job the actual time required should be entered.

3. *The student should list the operations in the order in which they should be performed.*

Different orders of procedure often are equally good. The pupil should be questioned as to his method and if he can give a good reason for it he should be permitted to follow his plan, altho it may not be the usual order

The teacher should never neglect this analysis and planning of the job. It is a matter of thought and reasoning and represents the highest type of development. The ability to do it is the thing that marks the distinction between the capable, self-reliant, high-grade mechanic and the low-grade journeyman who can do only the things he is told to do. It is quite different from acquiring information or developing manipulative skill, and to neglect it is to neglect one of the most important phases of the pupil's training.

4. *The instructor should give all necessary information and directions and, when necessary, give a demonstration of any new process involved.*

The manual gives very definite directions for performing the operations. The pupil should be required to read these directions very carefully before starting on his task and have them at hand for ready reference during the progress of the job. After a pupil has performed an operation a few times he will know *how* to do it and it will not be necessary for him to read the instructions unless he meets with some difficulty He will need practice, in order to acquire skill, long after he has learned how to perform the operations and no longer needs the instructions.

The teacher should demonstrate any difficult manipulative operation not made perfectly clear by the printed instructions. The most effective way of doing this is to have the pupil read the instructions or directions while the teacher performs the operation step by step as directed. This helps the pupil to realize the real value of the printed instructions.

The teacher should be sure that the pupil is familiar with the topics of information that may affect the success of the work.

5. *The work should be done according to plan.*

Having a definite and clearly understood plan with complete directions, the pupil should proceed with speed and decision to the doing of the job. Loitering, indecision, or careless and slovenly habits should never be permitted. The teacher should observe the work carefully and render assistance only where it is actually needed. The necessary material having been placed in the hands of the pupil, he should solve his problem unaided unless there is danger of his falling into bad habits.

6. *The teacher should check results.*

The teacher should observe the work carefully in order to determine the effectiveness of the instruction and whether additional practice is necessary in order to attain the desired skill. This gives an opportunity to talk with the pupil concerning the virtues or defects of his plan.

7 *Students should report on the job when completed.*

It is well to have students report to the group when the job is finished. The report should cover the following items:
    a) Time required to do the job.
    b) Material used on the job.
    c) Any special difficulties encountered and how they were overcome.
    d) Whether some other plan of procedure might have been better.

Such a report develops pride and a laudable ambition to excel in the matter of speed and workmanship. Also, some very valuable and helpful suggestions will be brought out in the discussion.

Every teacher of experience knows how difficult it is to get pupils to do the necessary preliminary study and planning of a job, and every teacher knows, also, that the failure to do this is one of the chief sources of unsatisfactory work. Planning a job requires careful, systematic thought and reasoning and most pupils prefer the more spectacular work of handling tools and materials. They are in a hurry to get at what to them is the real, creative work. It is difficult for them to realize that careful planning will mean a saving in time, energy and material. The teacher should invariably insist upon this conscious, definite planning until the habit is thoroly established. Such a habit will be an invaluable possession.

BUILDING AND MAINTAINING FORGE FIRE

Directions:

1. Clean the fire pot around the tuyere of all dirt and cinder Turn on the blast to blow small pieces out of the corners.

2. See that the tuyere fits tightly against the bottom of the fire pot.

3. Light a small amount of oily waste or a handful of shavings on the bottom, place it over the tuyere and cover this completely but lightly with small lumps of coke.

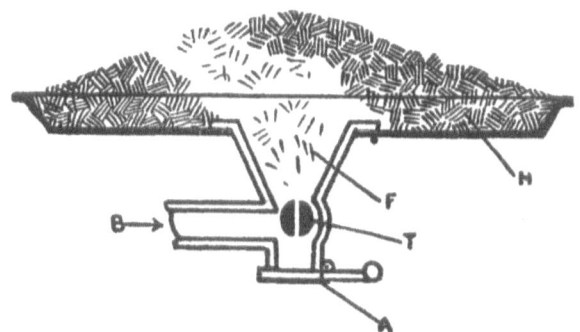

FIG. 1. Cross-section of forge and fire. H, hearth; F, fire pot; T, tuyere; B, blast; A, ash dump.

4. Apply a small amount of blast until the coke is converted into a live bed of coals.

5. Bank the fire on three sides with wet, green coal; leaving the side next to you open. Fig. 1.

6. The size of the pieces to be heated will determine the size of the fire used. Use a fire that will heat only that portion of the stock that is to be worked. For large work build up the fire until there is a heavy layer of coals covering the parts to be heated.

7 If a small fire is wanted and it tends to get too big, add wet coal on sides. If there is already sufficient fuel, pour water on the coke surrounding the fire.

8. When the fire becomes hollow, punch in coke from the sides.

9. After the fire has been used for a while, slag and cinder will form in the bottom over the tuyere. Remove this by pushing out the slag and cinder and build up the fire as before.

References:

Harcourt, *Elementary Forge Practice*, p. 17   Bacon, *Forge Practice*, p. 2.

Questions:

1. Why should a tuyere fit tightly against the bottom of the fire pot?
2. Why should the oily waste or shavings be covered with coke before the blast is turned on?
3. What is the effect of using too much blast when the fire is first started?
4. How is the blast distributed thru the fire?
5. What is green coal?
6. Why wet the green coal before it is put on the fire?
7. What will be the effect of getting the coal too wet?
8. Why is it necessary to have a compact fire?
9. Why is it impossible to heat iron quickly in a hollow, burned-out fire?
10. Why should a fire be kept as small as will adequately heat the work?
11. What is the effect on metal when it is heated in a burned-out or hollow fire?
12. Why should a fire be cleaned frequently of molten cinder?
13. What preparation of fire is necessary after removing slag and cinder?

Operation No. 2 15

HOLDING WORK

Directions:

1. Choose tongs wide enough in the throat to permit the jaws to be parallel when clamped on the work.

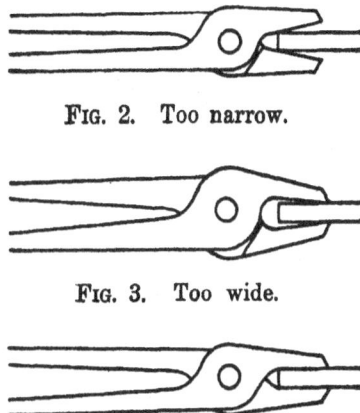

FIG. 2. Too narrow.

FIG. 3. Too wide.

FIG. 4. Correct.

2. If flat-jawed tongs fail to hold round work firmly, use bolt tongs.

3. If the jaws of the tongs when clamped are approximately parallel with the edges of the work but still the work is not held firmly, heat the tongs to a red heat and bend the jaws until they touch the stock along their entire length and hold it firmly.

4. If two pieces of stock are to be held in the same position with reference to each other, grasp the stock with the tongs, slip the link over the handles and force toward the jaws until the work is clamped firmly.

5. Keep the tongs cold by dipping them frequently in a slack tub.

6. Figs. 3, 4, 5, and 6 show common types of tongs. For special types of work use tongs designed for that particular kind of job. Figs. 7, 8, 9, and 10.

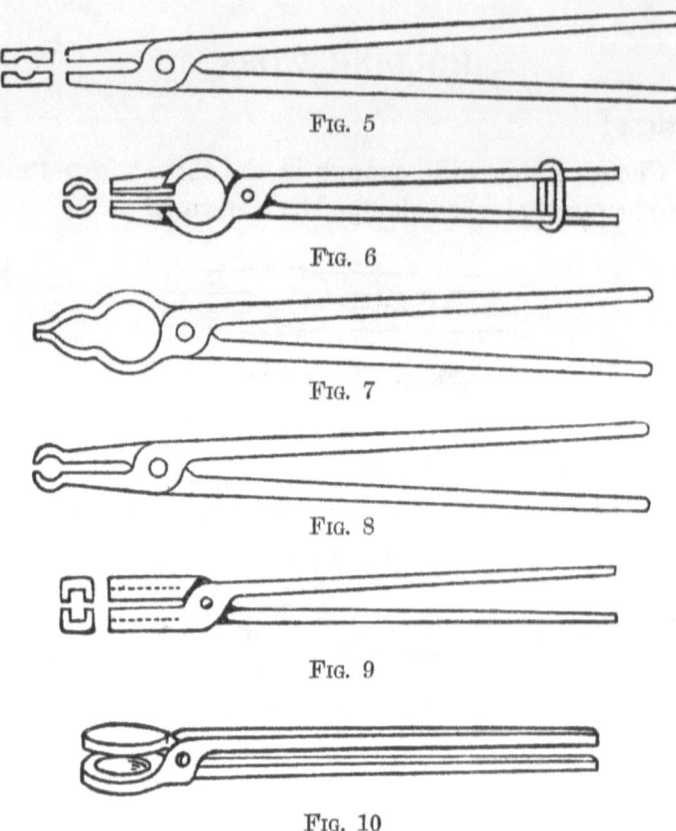

Fig. 5

Fig. 6

Fig. 7

Fig. 8

Fig. 9

Fig. 10

References:

Harcourt, *Elementary Forge Practice*, p. 23.   Bacon, *Forge Practice*, p. 13.

Questions:

1. Why is it necessary to handle stock with properly fitting tongs?
2. Should a pair of tongs that are manufactured to fit quarter-inch stock be forged to fit half-inch stock? Why?
3. Why should tongs be cooled frequently?
4. What is the purpose of the small groove on the inside of the jaws of flat-jawed tongs?
5. Why is it unsafe to use poorly fitting tongs?
6. What is the advantage of using tongs with short jaws for small work?

HEATING WORK

Directions:

1. Place the part of the stock to be heated in nearly a horizontal position in the center of the fire and arrange the coals with the poker until the part is surrounded with a bed of live coals. Be careful to prevent the blast from coming directly in contact with the stock. When the fire becomes hollow, punch in the sides with the poker

2. Use just enough blast to keep the fire burning well, and avoid too large a fire.

3. After the stock has been in the fire a short time, remove it to see how the heat is progressing.

4. If the heat is being taken on two pieces at the same time, as in the case of welding, and it is found that one piece is heating faster than the other remove from the fire the piece that is heating too fast and allow the other to catch up.

5. If a piece of stock is being heated that cannot be turned over in the fire, turn off the blast for a short time at intervals and allow the heat to soak thru until the temperature on both sides is uniform.

6. If large pieces are being worked, heat slowly so the stock will have a uniform temperature all the way thru.

References:

Harcourt, *Elementary Forge Practice*, p. 30. Bacon, *Forge Practice*, p. 17.

Questions:

1. Why keep the stock in nearly a horizontal position in the fire while heating?
2. Why does the stock heat more quickly in a compact fire than it does in a hollow one?
3. What is the effect of using too much blast?
4. What is the effect on the stock of being heated in a hollow fire?
5. What is the effect of having the blast come in direct contact with the stock while heating?
6. How can one prevent the draft from coming in direct contact with the stock?

MEASURING AND CUTTING STOCK

Directions:

1. Measure off on the bar the required length and mark with chalk at the point to be cut. If the stock is to be heated for cutting, mark also with a center punch or cold chisel, so the mark will not be lost when heated.

2. For curves and irregular shapes the experienced smith usually relies upon his judgment as to the amount of stock required unless a rather high degree of accuracy is necessary, but this is not a safe plan for beginners. In order to develop this ability, however, it is well to make an estimate of the stock required, mark lightly with chalk, and then check this measurement by actual measurement.

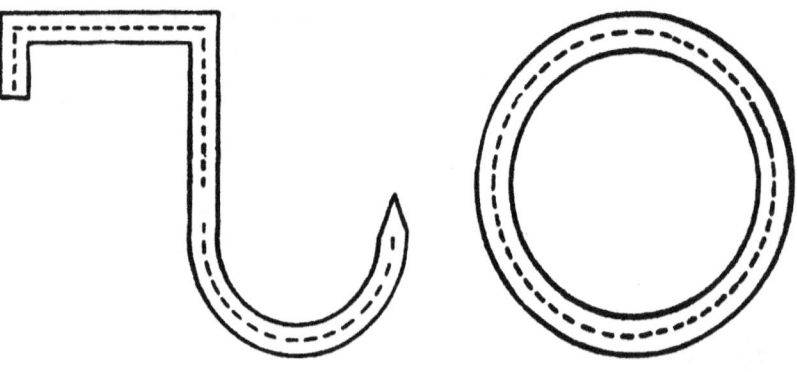

FIG. 11. The dotted line is the measuring line.   FIG. 12

3. In bending stock, the outside of the stock on the curve stretches and the inside part is compressed. There is a neutral line at the center that is neither stretched nor compressed. The proper length of stock for any bent shape may be found by measuring this center line of the curve or bend. Probably the best way to measure this line is to take a small wire that will bend readily and keep its shape, and lay it on the central

Operation No. 4
Page No. 2

line. Then straighten the wire and measure it. If a weld is to be made, allowance must be made for upsetting. Fig. 11.

4. The length required for rings or bands may be calculated by taking three times the inside diameter plus four times the thickness of the stock, or by taking three and one-seventh times the diameter of the center line plus one-half the diameter of the stock. Fig. 12.

5. Cut wrought-iron and soft steel under ⅜" in diameter by placing it on the hardy and striking with the hammer directly over the cutting edge. When the cut is two-thirds thru, bend back and forth until it breaks off. If the cut is to be finished on the hardy, strike on the far side of the cutting edge when it is nearly finished. Fig. 13.

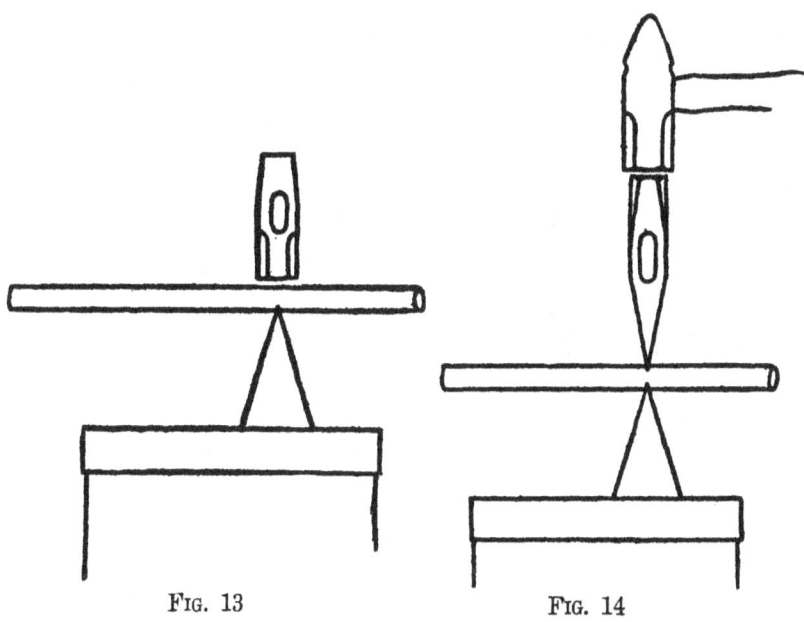

Fig. 13   Fig. 14

6. If tool steel, or wrought-iron over ⅜" in diameter, is to be cut, place the stock on the edge of the anvil where the cut is to be made and set the cutter on the top of the stock exactly even with the cutting edge of the hardy and strike with the sledge until the stock may be easily broken. Fig. 14.

7 Always heat the tool steel to a low red before attempting to cut it. Heavy stock may be more readily cut when heated.

8. If the cut is to be made in flat stock or for a considerable length in sheet stock, lay the portion where the cut is to be made flat on the anvil and make the cut two-thirds of the way thru the stock. Place the nearly finished cut so that it lies along the edge of the anvil. Place the cutter on the far end of the cut with the handle elevated to about forty-five degrees, the lower corner of the cutter extending beyond the stock and resting against the side of the anvil, thus forming a shear Cut along the edge of the anvil until the cut is finished. Fig. 15.

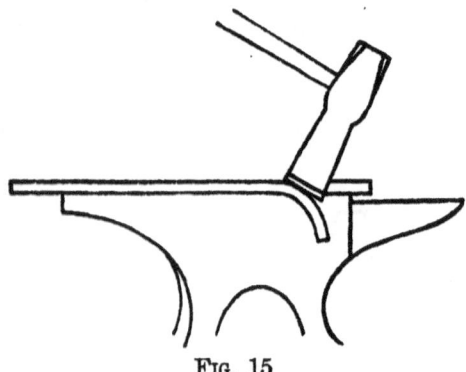

FIG. 15

References:

Bacon, *Forge Practice*, p. 41. Harcourt, *Elementary Forge Practice*, p. 33.

Questions:

1. When cutting stock on the hardy, why strike on the far side of the cutting edge when the cut is nearly thru?
2. Why is it faster to use a hardy in connection with the cutter in making the cut?
3. What is the advantage of heating the stock before making the cut?
4. Why is it necessary to heat tool steel before cutting?
5. How does the form of a hot cutter differ from that of a cold cutter?
6. Why is the cold cutter tempered while the hot cutter is not?

Operation No. 5

DRAWING OUT STOCK

Directions:

1. Heat the stock to a bright red and place it on the anvil so that the hammer blows will fall near the center of the anvil face. Deliver blows so that the face of the hammer will fall approximately parallel to the face of the anvil. Between blows turn the stock so that the blows fall alternately on the sides and the top, keeping the work square in section.

2. If the stock tends to become diamond shaped, tilt it on the long diagonal and deliver drawing blows so that the stock is drawn back square in section. If the stock is sufficiently large, place it in the corner between the chipping block and the face of the anvil while delivering drawing blows as above directed. Fig 16.

FIG. 16

3. If the stock is to be drawn to a point, raise the handles of the tongs and draw the stock to a blunt point, keeping the point of the stock even with the far edge of the anvil. To finish the taper, lower the tong handles and deliver blows so that the face of the hammer will form the angle of the taper desired with the face of the anvil. If the stock is to be drawn to a round taper draw it to a square taper first, then octagon and finally round. Fig. 17

4. To do rapid drawing, heat the stock and place it across the horn of the anvil and strike heavy blows with the hammer so the horn will form a series of notches on the stock. Smooth

with the hammer This series of notches may be made over the bottom fuller instead of the horn or made with the top and the bottom fuller with the aid of a striker. Fig. 18.

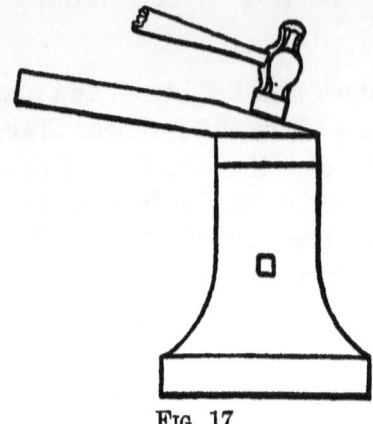

FIG. 17

5. If Norway iron is being used the stock must be at a white heat while the point is being made.

6. Draw tool steel at a red heat.

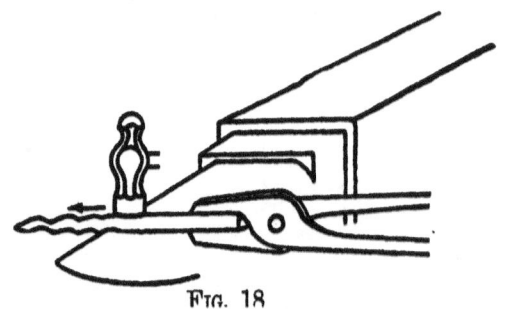

FIG. 18

References:

Bacon, *Forge Practice*, p. 51.

Questions:

1. Why turn the stock thru ninety degrees between blows?
2. What is the advantage of first squaring the stock if it is to be drawn to a point?
3. Why should Norway iron be kept to a white heat if it is to be drawn to a point?
4. Why does a series of notches tend to increase the length rather than the width?
5. What is the cause of the stock's splitting when being drawn?
6. In drawing to a point why make a blunt point first?

Operation No. 6

BENDING ROUND AND RECTANGULAR STOCK

Directions

1. Heat uniformly the stock to be bent. If a curve or complete circle is to be made, extend the end of the heated stock over the horn of the anvil and deliver glancing blows beyond the horn, so that the curve is started exactly at the end of the stock. As the stock cools it bends with difficulty and should be reheated.

2. If the stock becomes curved too much, place one end of the curve on the horn and curve up. Hold the other end in the tongs and deliver glancing blows on top of the curve between the tongs and the horn.

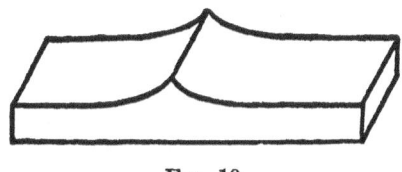

FIG. 19

3. If a right angle bend is to be formed having both the inside and outside corners sharp, then the stock must be upset thru the portion that is to form the bend to about one and one-half times its original thickness. Make the bend over the sharp edge of the face of the anvil and use drawing blows to pull excess stock out into the outside corner. Fig. 19.

4. When bending flat stock edgewise and the inside circumference tends to buckle, the stock must be placed on the anvil face and hammered flat frequently

5. If thin, flat stock cannot be bent by the above method and uniform thickness is not essential, hammer on the outside edge of the stock until the proper curve is formed.

6. Make a slight curve in thin stock by peening the outside edge.

7 Straighten thin stock by peening inside edge.

References:

Ilgen, *Forge Work*, p. 67.   Bacon, *Forge Practice*, p. 59.

Questions:
1. Why should glancing blows be delivered when bending round stock?
2. Why should blows be delivered to either one side or the other of the horn rather than directly on top when bending?
3. Why is it necessary to upset the stock first in forming corners?
4. Why does flat stock buckle during the process of bending edgewise?
5. Why does peening the outside edge of stock tend to curve it?

Operation No. 7

BENDING EYES

Directions:

1. Measure off and mark with a center punch the amount of stock required to form the eye. Heat to a bright red and bend the stock to a sharp right angle at the point marked.

2. Extend the end of the stock that is to form the eye over the tip of the anvil horn and bend it until it is approximately the curvature of the finished eye. Fig. 20.

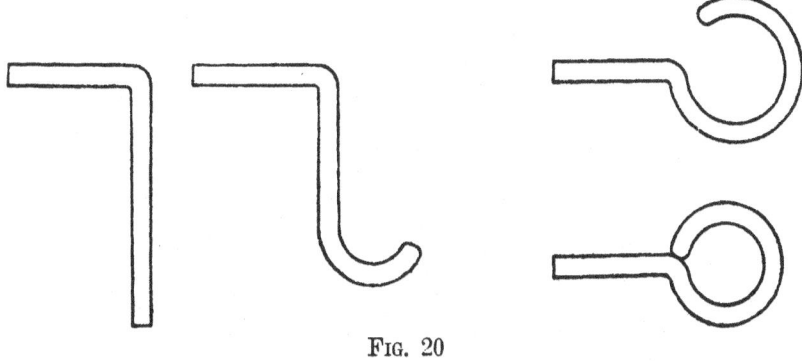

FIG. 20

3. As the proper curve is formed, keep slipping the stock over the horn, striking glancing blows until all the stock back to a right-angle bend has been formed into a circle.

4. If the eye is not circular, slip it over the horn as far as it will go and strike lightly until it is perfectly round. Fig. 21.

5. Grasp the eye in the tongs and lay the shank on the anvil face, with the opening of the eye up and the eye pressed closely against the corner of the anvil. In this position, hammer until the shank is perfectly straight. This tends to reduce curvature at the right-angle bend.

6. If the eye is not central with respect to the shank, either put in or take out the curve where the first right-angle bend was formed.

7 To put in the curve, hook the eye over the tip of the horn with the opening down, holding the shank in the tongs;

strike blows with the cross peen of the hammer on the original right-angle bend.

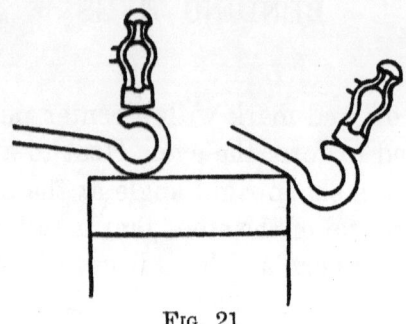

FIG. 21

References:

Ilgen, *Forge Work*, p. 49.   Bacon, *Forge Practice*, p. 54.

Questions:

1. Why is it necessary to bend the stock first to a right angle?
2. Why is it necessary to begin at the end of the stock to make a curve?
3. What will happen if we hammer too much on the outside of the circle when we true it over the horn?
4. Why is it necessary to retain the right-angle bend until the eye is completely formed?
5. How much ⅜ inch stock would be required to bend an eye of 1 inch inside diameter?

Operation No. 8

TWISTING

Directions.

1. Mark with a center punch the ends of the part of the stock to be twisted. Heat to a uniformly bright red.

2. If the length of the twist is more than two inches and the stock is under a half inch square, clamp the stock firmly with two pairs of close-fitting tongs, the edges of the jaws even with the center punch marks, and the part to be twisted between the tongs. Rotate until the required twist is made, being careful to keep the stock in line.

3. If the stock is heavy or if the length to be twisted is more than two inches, clamp the stock in the vise at one end of the part to be twisted. Clamp with a monkey wrench at the other end of the twist and rotate the wrench until the required twist is made, being careful to keep the stock in line.

4. Cool the part twisting too fast by pouring on a small stream of water from an oil-can or cup, and continue twisting.

5. When the stock is uniformly twisted straighten with a wooden mallet on a block of wood.

References:

Harcourt, *Elementary Forge Practice*, p. 34. Ilgen, *Forge Work*, p. 45. Bacon, *Forge Practice*, p. 66.

Questions:
 1. Why use close-jawed tongs in twisting stock?
 2. What are the causes of uneven twisting of stock?
 3. Why use a wooden mallet in straightening the twist?
 4. Why use the vise instead of the tongs when long lengths of twist are to be made?
 5. What is the effect of twisting on the length of the stock?

UPSETTING

Directions

1. Heat the part that is to be upset to a white heat and place it on anvil, hot end down. Deliver heavy blows on the cold end, being careful to keep the stock at right angles to the face of anvil. When the stock bends, straighten it immediately. Correct any irregularity by placing it flat on the face of the anvil and hammering until the upset portion is symmetrical.

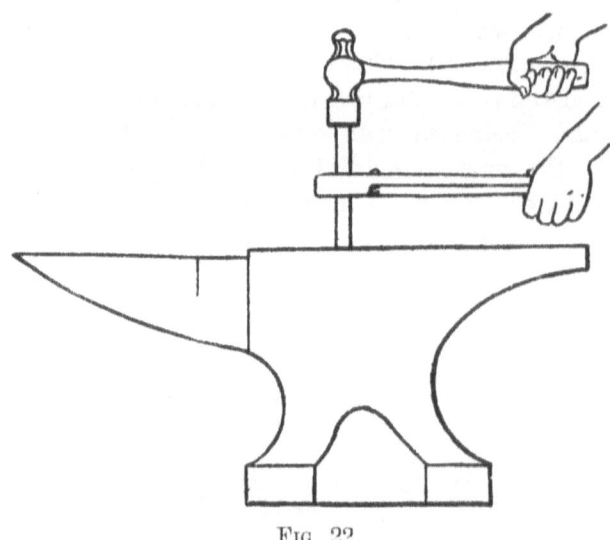

Fig. 22

2. If the stock tends to upset in other than the one desired place, cool the parts that should not be upset.
3. If large, long pieces of stock are to be upset, heat to white heat the part to be upset and ram against the face or side of the anvil or floor plate.
4. Light blows tend to upset the stock only on the end (Fig. 23 , heavy blows tend to upset thru a greater length (Fig. 24)

Operation No. 9
Page No. 2

If the end of stock tends to upset too much, cool it slightly and deliver heavy blows.

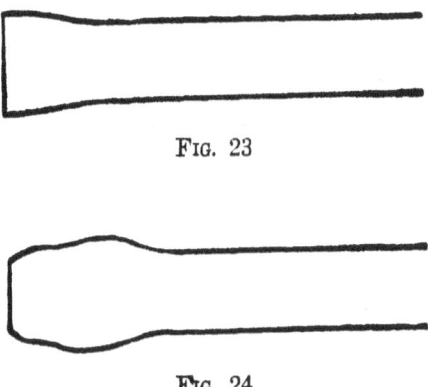

Fig. 23

Fig. 24

References:
 Ilgen, *Forge Work*, p. 41.   Bacon, *Forge Practice*, p. 55.

Questions:
1. Why do we place stock on the anvil hot end down to upset?
2. What is the purpose of upsetting stock?
3. Why do light blows tend to upset the stock at the end?
4. What is the effect on the stock of attempting to upset it when at too low heat?

HEADING

Directions

1. Upset the stock sufficiently for a head of the required size. This usually will require that the stock be upset until it is shortened by about three times the thickness of the head.

2. Heat upset stock to nearly a white heat, and place it in a heading tool slightly larger than the diameter of the original stock. Fig. 25.

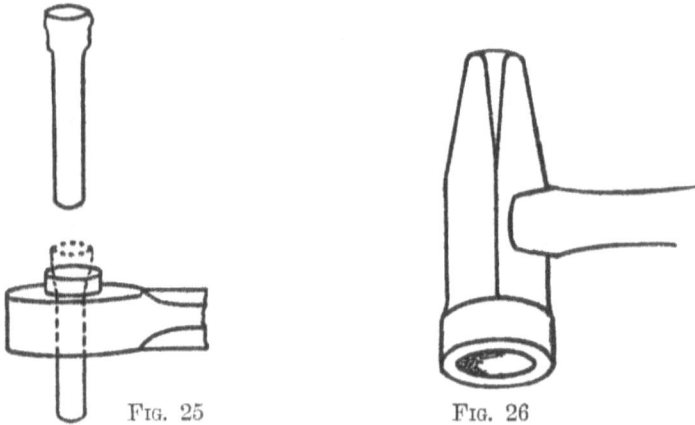

Fig. 25   Fig. 26

3. Extend the shank thru the hardy-hole in the face of the anvil and deliver heavy blows on top of the stock, extending above the face of heading tool, being careful to form the head as nearly on the center of the shank as possible.

4. Hammer until the head is about one and one-half times the thickness that it is to be when finished, then remove it from the heading tool by turning it upside down on the face of the anvil, and lifting the heading tool off, leaving the bolt standing on the face of the anvil, head down.

5. Grasp the shank of the bolt with the tongs, and hold it on the anvil with the shank parallel to the face of the anvil. Hammer on the sides of the bolt head until they are approximately parallel with the edges of the shank.

6. Place the bolt on the anvil again, head down, and examine it to determine whether or not the head is on the center

7 If the shank is found to be nearer one side of the head than the other, proceed as follows Reheat it to a bright red, place it in the heading tool with the narrow edge of the head to the right, extend the shank thru the hardy-hole and deliver a heavy drawing blow on the left or wide edge, of the head, with the hammer face forming an approximate forty-five degree angle with the face of the anvil. Continue to deliver drawing blows, meanwhile lowering the hammer handle until the face of the hammer and the face of the anvil are approximately parallel, and the head is exactly on the center

Caution: Never continue to hammer the head until it becomes thinner than it is to be when finished.

8. Hammer alternately on the sides of the head and top until the edges are parallel to the shank. Continue until the corners of the head come out perfectly sharp and the head is perfectly round and of a uniform thickness; then square the head.

9. To form a square head, continue to hammer alternately on the sides and top until the head is uniformly square, uniformly thick, and the corners come out perfectly sharp and of the required width and thickness.

10. Finish the top of the head by placing a buttonhead set, Fig. 26, on the top and hammering until the arch is formed on all sides from corner to corner. Hammer the edges until they are again parallel to the shank.

11. If a hexagon head is to be formed, the operations are exactly the same, except that, in treating the stock after it is perfectly round, it is turned thru sixty instead of ninety degrees while being forged.

References:

Harcourt, *Elementary Forge Practice*, p. 73. Bacon, *Forge Practice*, p. 79.

Questions:

1. What would be the result of hammering the head too thin when it is put thru the heading tool the first time?

2. Why is it necessary to keep the stock at a high heat when upsetting it in the heading tool?

3. Why should the heading tool be slightly larger than the stock being worked?

4. Which side of the heading tool should be placed down? Why?

5. Is the heading tool the same size at both ends?

6. Why is it important to have the shank slip loosely thru the heading tool up to the upset position?

7 During the process of upsetting the stock in the heading tool, how can you determine whether the head is off the center without removing it from the heading tool?

Operation No. 11 33

PUNCHING

Directions:

1. Heat the stock to a bright red and place it flat on the anvil. If the tool steel is being punched, heat it to a slightly lower temperature.

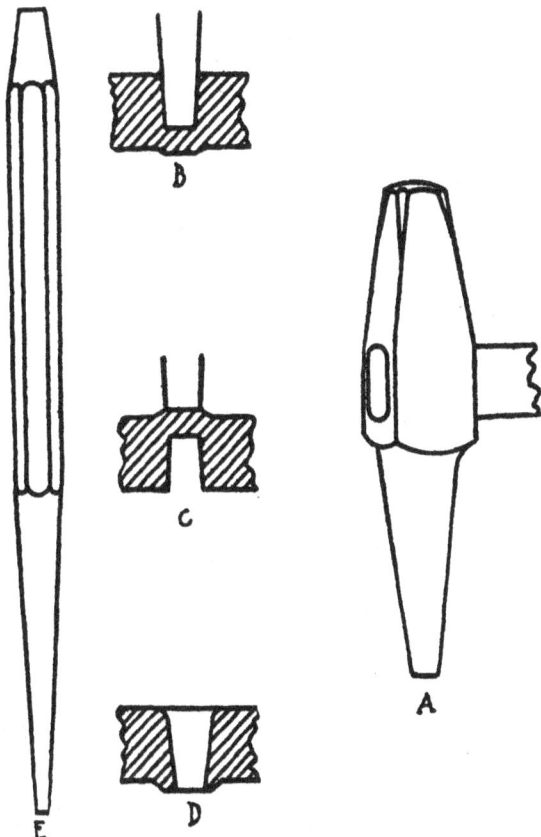

FIG. 27

2. Place the punch *A*, Fig. 27, on the stock as near the spot where the hole is to be made as possible. If the punch is not exactly in position, lean it slightly and twist it until the end of it is exactly where the hole is to be made.

3. Hold the punch in a vertical position and deliver a heavy blow Then quickly drive the punch about two-thirds of the way thru or until it drives with difficulty B, Fig. 27

4. Remove the punch and turn the stock over quickly. Place the punch on the punch print, C, Fig. 27, and drive it thru.

5. Place the stock over the hardy-hole or pritchel hole and drive the punch thru from each side alternately until the hole is the desired size. D, Fig. 27.

6. If the punch tends to stick when being driven thru the stock, remove the punch and put a little oxide of iron from the anvil block in the hole. If the punch still sticks, it indicates that it is upsetting in the hole. Remove it, draw it down, and cool it before continuing.

References:

Harcourt, *Elementary Forge Practice*, p. 35.

Questions:

1. Why is the first blow delivered on the punch a heavy one?
2. Why should we drive the punch thru as quickly as possible?
3. What is the cause of the punch upsetting in the hole during the process of punching and how can it be avoided?
4. When the stock is turned over, how is the location of the hole on the other side determined?

Operation No. 12

FORMING PUNCHED EYE

Directions

1. Heat the stock to a light-red heat and upset the end of the stock to one and one-half times its original diameter and to a distance from the end equal to twice the diameter of the stock.

2. Tilt the stock on the face of the anvil to an angle of about thirty degrees and flatten the opposite corners of the upset end at two points. Fig. 28.

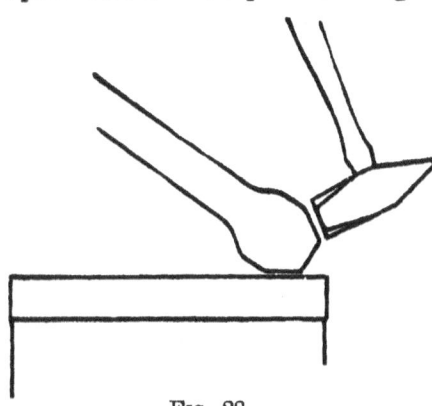

Fig. 28

3. Lay the stock flat on the face of the anvil at right angles to the flattened corners and make a taper, one end of which is the required thickness of the eye, and the other end the thickness of the original stock, and as long as it is wide. Fig. 29.

4. Place the tapered end on the fuller with the edges of the taper in a vertical position; and extend over the fuller enough stock to form roughly a circle when the fuller marks

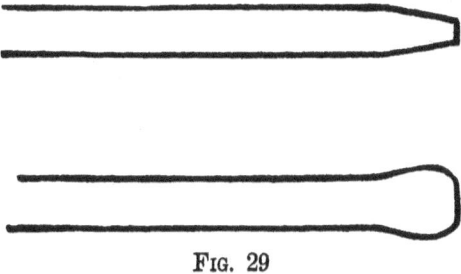

Fig. 29

are made. Place the top fuller on the stock directly over the bottom fuller and make the fuller marks on the edge of the stock until the neck under the eye is slightly larger than it is to be when finished. Fig. 30.

5. Extend the stock across the face of the anvil until the fullered notch rests on the far edge of the anvil.

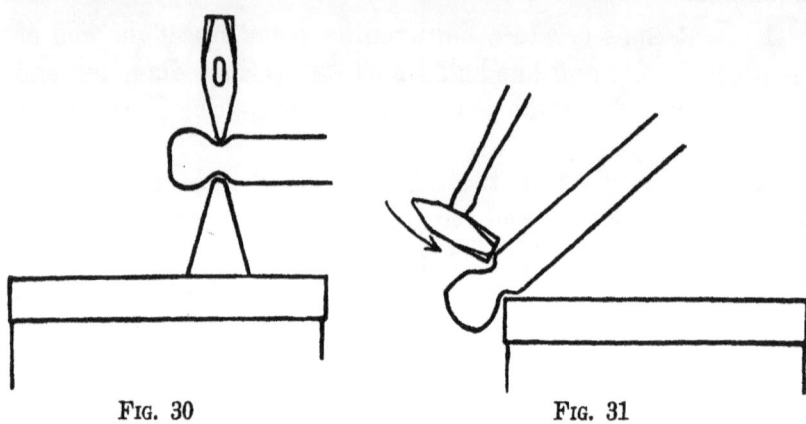

FIG. 30   FIG. 31

6. Tilt slightly and with the hammer draw down the shank under the eye until the required length of taper is formed, being careful not to form a cold shut just under the eye. Fig. 31.

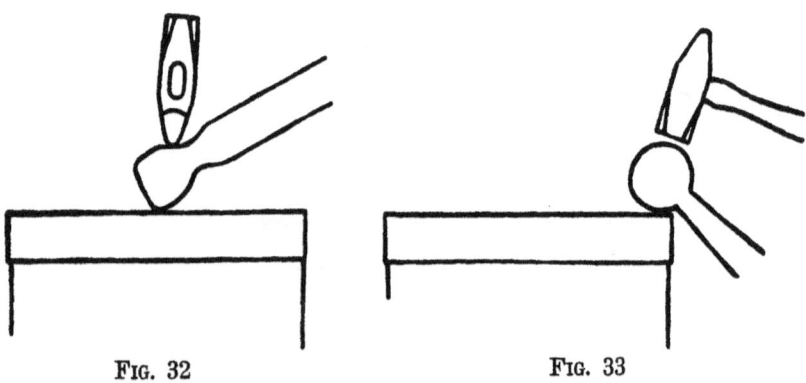

FIG. 32   FIG. 33

7 If the stock has been insufficiently upset make fuller marks slightly farther from the end so that the stock to form the eye will be somewhat elongated instead of circular Hook the fullered notch on the tip of the horn and deliver a heavy blow on the end. Turn the stock over and deliver another

blow on the end. Continue turning between blows until the stock has the general outline of a circle.

8. Take the sharp corners off the stock just under the eye with the fuller until the lower part of the eye is circular. Draw the taper down perfectly smooth under the eye. Fig. 32.

9. Turn the eye portion on the edge and hammer around the circumference until it is perfectly round. Fig. 33.

Fig. 34

10. Lay the stock flat on the anvil and punch the eye.

11. Place the hole on the tip of the horn and round the corners of the stock forming the eye by swinging the tongs out during the rounding process until they form a 45 degree angle with the horn. Fig. 34.

12. Turn the stock over and round the corners on the other side.

13. Continue working first on one side then the other until the stock in the eye is circular in section.

References:

Harcourt, *Elementary Forge Practice,* p. 60. Bacon, *Forge Practice,* p. 71.

Questions:

1. What should be the diameter of the punch with respect to the width of the eye blank?

2. What should be the thickness of the eye blank with respect to the width?

3. Why swing the stock at a 45 degree angle while rounding the stock in the eye.

4. What precautions are necessary in order to prevent increasing the size of the eye while rounding it?

5. Why bevel the corners of stock at a 60 degree angle before flattening for the eye.

6. What causes a cold shut?

FULLERING

Directions:

1. Choose the top and bottom fullers that will cut the required size groove in the stock.

2. Place the bottom fuller in the hardy hole so that the top edge is lengthwise of the anvil.

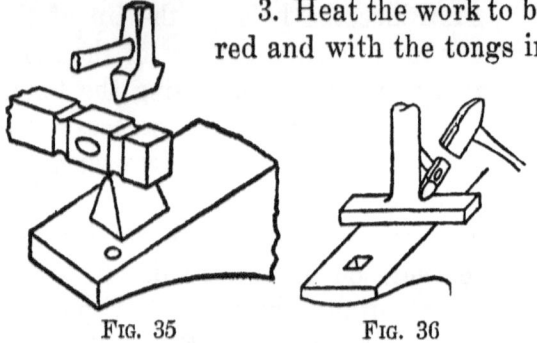

Fig. 35   Fig. 36

3. Heat the work to be fullered to a bright red and with the tongs in the left hand place the stock on the bottom fuller Hold the top fuller directly over the bottom fuller, Fig. 35, and have the helper strike medium heavy blows.

4. Raise the top fuller between the blows of the sledge, and turn the work over frequently so that the top fuller will not cut on the same side of the stock all the time.

5. Continue until the groove is cut to the required depth.

6. If the groove is to be cut on one side only lay the work on the anvil and use the top fuller

7 When forming a square shoulder with the fuller, slant the top of it slightly away from the shoulder   Fig. 36.

References:

Bacon, *Forge Practice*, p. 83.

Questions:

1. Why place the bottom fuller with the edge lengthwise of the anvil?
2. Why is it necessary to have the top fuller directly over the bottom fuller before the first blow of the sledge is struck?
3. Why should the work be turned over occasionally?
4. What effect will fullering have on the length of the stock?
5. When cutting the groove on one side only of the work why use the top fuller instead of the bottom?

Operation No. 14

SWAGING

Directions:

1. Choose a top and bottom swage of the required size, and place the bottom swage in hardy-hole with the groove crosswise of the anvil.

2. Heat the part of the stock to be swaged to a bright red heat and with the tongs in the left hand place the work in the groove of the bottom swage. Place the top swage on the work directly over the bottom swage, holding the handle in the right hand and have the helper strike medium heavy blows with the sledge.

3. Between blows turn the work in the groove and remove the top swage to see what effect the blow has had.

4. Continue until the stock is of uniform shape and of the size required. Fig. 37

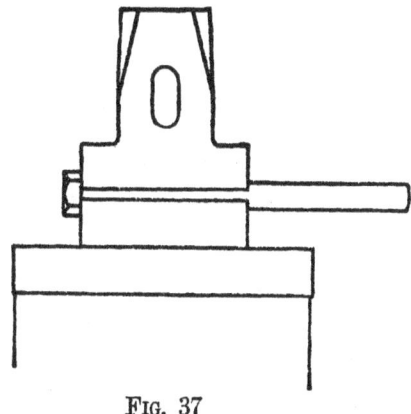

FIG. 37

5. If swaging is to be done against a shoulder, as in the case of a bolt, place the shoulder against the bottom swage, place the top swage on the work and tilt the top of it slightly toward the shoulder. In this position have the helper strike medium heavy blows.

6. Finish swaging at a dull red heat.

7 For special shapes use the large floor swage block.

References:

Ilgen, *Forge Work*, p. 17

Questions:

    1. Why place the bottom swage so the groove is crosswise of the anvil?
    2. Why should the work be turned while being swaged?
    3. Why finish the work at a dull red heat?
    4. Why tilt the top swage toward the shoulder when swaging against a shoulder?
    5. What would be the effect of tilting the top swage too much toward the shoulder?

Operation No. 15 41

STRIKING

Directions:

1. Grasp the sledge handle with both hands, one about six inches and the other about eighteen inches from the hammer

2. Stand close to the anvil on the opposite side from and facing the blacksmith.

3. If you strike right handed extend your right foot about a half step in front of the left one. If you strike left handed extend the left foot.

4. Watch the blacksmiths' hammer for signals. He will strike the work lightly at the point where he wishes you to strike.

5. Begin striking with medium heavy blows, raising the sledge thru a distance that will give the required force to the blow.

6. When the blow is delivered draw the sledge quickly toward you before starting to raise it.

7 If the blacksmith strikes heavy blows on the work it indicates that you are to deliver heavy blows with the sledge.

8. Always strike the work in the same place and at the same angle as the smith is striking it.

9. When the smith taps the anvil rapidly with his hammer cease striking.

Questions:

1. Why should one of the striker's feet be extended while striking?
2. Why should the sledge be raised only a short distance above instead of being swung over the shoulder?
3. Why pull the sledge slightly toward you after delivering the blow?

WELDING

Directions:

1. Clean the fire of all cinder and slag that may be collected over the tuyere. Have a good supply of coke so that the fire may be replenished without using green coal. Large work requires a deep fire and a large bed of coals and if such work is being done, construct the fire accordingly

2. Clean the face of the anvil of all scale, place the hammer in a position so that the handle may be easily grasped, and place the anvil in a convenient position with reference to the forge so that the weld may be completed without delay after the heat is taken.

3. Place the work to be welded in the fire in an approximately horizontal position with a live bed of coals between the work and the tuyere and the part to be welded directly over the tuyere.

4. Cover the work with a bed of live coals and start the blast. Take the heat slowly Turn the stock over occasionally while the heat is being taken. This is especially important on large work. If one part heats faster than the other, turn off the blast and let the stock soak until it is of a uniform temperature thruout.

5. Pull the stock out occasionally or uncover it with a poker to see how the heat is progressing. When the stock is a bright red, sprinkle a small amount of flux on the scarf. After this is done replace it in the fire quickly and recover it so that the stock will not be exposed to air any longer than necessary

6. Continue to heat the stock until the dry, scaly appearance caused by the oxidation of the metal becomes molten looking and fluid iron is actually flowing on the surface. As soon as this condition exists remove it from the fire, strike the work on the anvil, place the scarfs together and hammer, *first*

Operation No. 16
Page No. 2

with very light blows, then with heavier ones, until the pieces are firmly united.

7 Do not attempt to stick the pieces together by hammer-

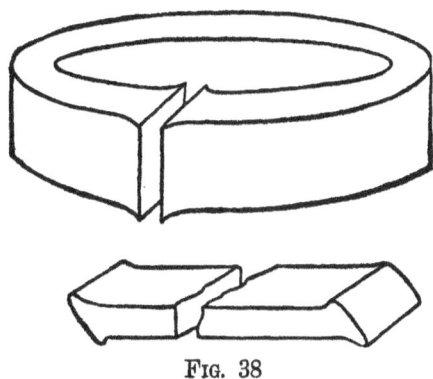

FIG. 38

ing after they have cooled below the welding heat.

8. If the pieces fail to stick at the first heat, cut off the tips and resurface the scarfs before trying again.

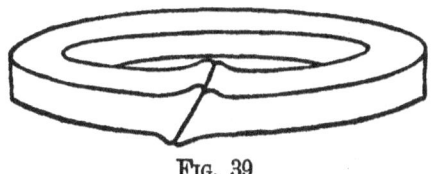

FIG. 39

9. Make welds with as few heats as possible as the difficulty of getting iron or steel to stick increases with the number of heats. Figs. 38 and 39.

Lap Weld.

10. If an ordinary lap weld is to be made, as in the case of a flat ring, heat and upset the ends of the stock thruout the length that will become red hot during the process of welding until it is one and one-half times its original diameter or thickness. Place the stock flat on the face of the anvil and with the edge of the face of the hammer scarf or bevel the end of the stock until it forms a 45 degree angle. Deliver blows so that the center of the scarf will be somewhat rounded instead of hollow Next, place it on edge and draw the bevel

molten on the surfaces have the helper remove one piece of the stock from the fire, strike it on the anvil to knock off the slag, and place it flat on the anvil so that the end is about even with the center of the anvil. While the helper is doing this, remove the other piece from the fire, strike it on the anvil and place it end to end with the piece held by the

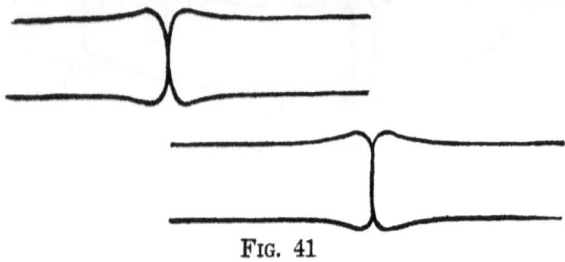

Fig. 41

helper. Caution should be given to the helper to hold the stock firmly Deliver blows on the end of the piece you are holding until the pieces are firmly united, and the crack between the ends is about closed. Then deliver blows on the top of the weld until it is perfectly smooth. Draw or swage it down to original dimensions.

Split or Cleft Weld.

14. If a split or cleft weld is to be made, heat and upset the stock as far as it will become red, during the process of welding and until each piece is about one and one-half times its original diameter. Clamp one piece of stock firmly in the vise and split the end for a distance equal to the original diameter of the stock. Spread the ends until they form a Y and draw the sides of the Y until they are blunt edged and form an oval shaped point. Make a blunt taper on the ends of the other piece, forming a 60 degree angle between the surfaces of the taper Figs. 42 and 43.

Roughen the surfaces of the taper with a chisel or the edge of the hammer Heat to a red heat and sprinkle flux on the ends and drive the taper into a Y and bend the ends of the Y down over the bulge on the taper piece to prevent the pieces from coming apart. Build up the fire so that the stock will lie on a live bed of coals with no strain on the parts to be welded. Place the stock in the fire and take the heat slowly, meanwhile turning it over and over, so that the larger portions will become heated as fast as the tips of the Y

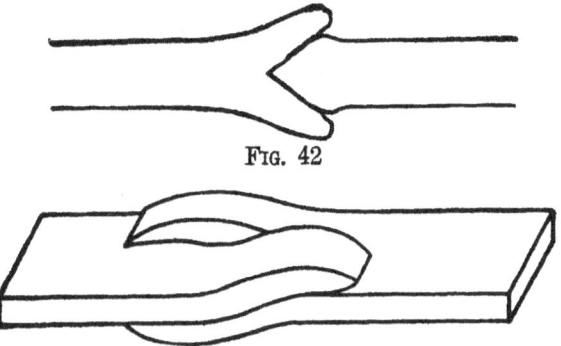

FIG. 42

FIG. 43. Split weld for thin stock.

Turn off the blast occasionally to allow the pieces to assume a uniform temperature thruout. When all is at uniform welding heat, remove the work from the fire, having the helper support one end to keep it in line, and place it flat on the anvil. While the helper is holding one end of the stock, deliver one blow on the other end of the piece to drive the wedge firmly into the Y; then with light blows weld down the ends of the Y over the bulge. Next, deliver blows around the weld until the pieces are firmly united. In case of welding tool steel or mild steel, as in pointing tools, it is sometimes advisable to heat the pieces separately because of the different welding temperatures of the two materials.

Chain Links.

15. If chain links are being welded, bend the pieces of stock into U-forms. Heat the ends of the sides of the U to a bright red heat and place it on the sharp edge of the anvil just above the chipping block, with the outside of the edge of the left side of the U coming exactly even with the sharp edge of the anvil, and the sides of the U forming a 45 degree angle with the horn; the other side of the U extending over the face of the anvil. Fig. 44. In this position strike a flat

blow on the part resting on the edge of the anvil. Continue to strike blows, meanwhile moving the handles of the tongs toward you until the side of the U is parallel with the edge and slips off. Turn the stock over and repeat the operations on the other end of the U Heat and bend the ends together until the link is somewhat pointed, the thick outside corner coinciding and the inside corners resting near the middle of the width of the opposite scarf. Grasp the opposite end of the link and place in the fire. Keep turning the link from side to side so that the heat will be uniform. When the stock becomes molten-ooking, remove it from the fire, place it flat on the anvil and deliver light blows. Turn the link over quickly and deliver a blow on the other side. Then place it over the tip of the horn and hammer on the corners until the stock is round in cross-section thru the weld. Figs. 46 and 47

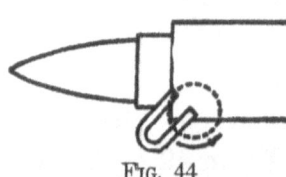
Fig. 44

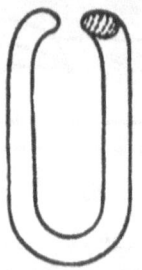

Fig. 45

T Weld.

16. Heat to a bright red heat the top of the T where the leg of the T is to be welded on, and upset it until it is about one and one-half times its original thickness; and if it is flat stock, until it is slightly wider also. Heat the leg of the T on the end and upset a similar amount.

17. In the case of flat stock, place the bar of the T flat on the anvil and with the peen of a ball-peen hammer scarf it by forming a 45 degree taper on one side, as wide as the leg of the T and at the place where the upsetting was done. Fig. 46. Draw with the peen until the point of the scarf extends slightly past the edge of the stock and forms an egg-shaped point.

18. Place the leg of the T flat on the anvil and scarf the upset end to a 45 degree angle, turn it on edge, raise the cold

end, and hammer the scarf to an oval-shaped point. Place the back flat on the anvil and hammer it with the corner of the hammer until the scarfed surface is slightly convex, being careful to prevent the entire length of the scarf from exceeding one and one-half times the original thickness.

19. Place the pieces in a clean fire with the scarf up, and slowly raise the heat to a bright red. Remove, flux, replace it in the fire, and raise to a welding heat. Before removing the weld from the fire, turn the pieces over so that the scarf is down for a few seconds; then turn the blast off. Wait for a few seconds, remove the stock from the fire, strike on the anvil and place the bar of the T lengthwise of the anvil, scarf

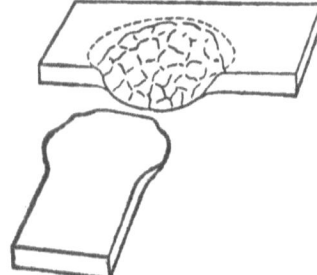
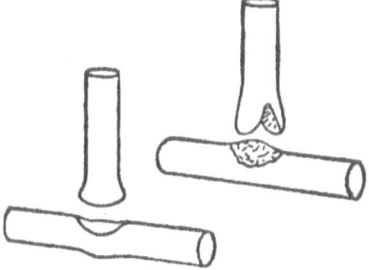

FIG. 46. T-weld in flat stock.   FIG. 47. T-weld in round stock.

up. Rest the leg of the T on the edge of the anvil and the lower end onto the bar. Strike very light blows at first, then heavy, and continue until the pieces are firmly united. Place the weld over the edge of the anvil occasionally to true the corners between the leg and the bar.

20. If a T-weld is to be made in round stock upset the pieces as in the case of flat stock. Prepare the scarf on the bar of the T with the peen of the hammer, fuller, or bob punch. Scarf the end of the leg of the T to fit the scarf on the bar, Fig. 47. Proceed to weld as in the case of flat stock. Use a top fuller to weld down corners and projections. Finish with swage blocks. A T-weld in round stock may be made also by splitting the end of the stem of the T and proceeding the same way as in a cleft weld.

Welding Eye.

21. Heat the end of the stock to a bright red heat and form a rectangular taper, the length of which is about twice the thickness of the stock. Hammer the end of this taper to a blunt point slightly wider than it is thick.

22. Bend all of the taper over the edge of the anvil to an angle of about 20 degrees. Fig. 48.

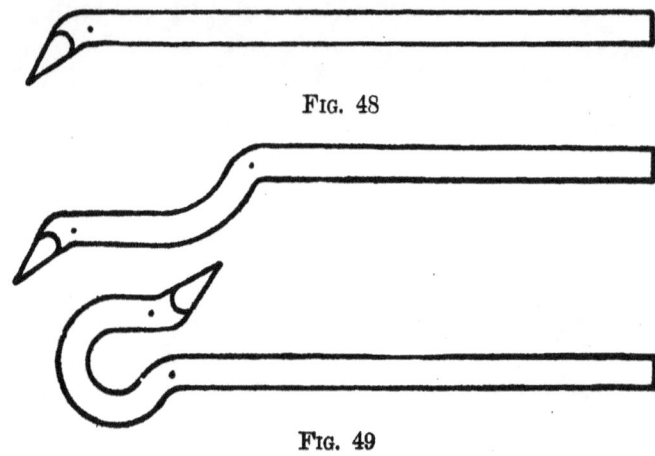

Fig. 48

Fig. 49

23. Mark with a center punch the length of the stock required to form the eye. Heat at the mark and extend the stock over the end of the horn of the anvil with the front of the taper down. Fig. 49.

24. In this position put approximately a right angle bend in the stock by striking the stock just beyond the point where it rests on the anvil.

25. Place the stock near the tip of the horn so that the taper extends just past the horn and is inclined upward. With the work in this position strike glancing blows just beyond the horn and push the work forward as it is bent until all of the stock that was bent to a right angle is formed into a circle and the full length of the taper rests on the shank of the eye, and the butt end of the taper rests at the center punch mark. Bend the taper until it lies centrally along the stock. Fig. 50.

Operation No. 16   51
Page No. 10

26. Place the stock in the fire with the eye extending thru the fire and taper coming directly over the tuyere. When it is red hot remove and flux.

27. Replace it in the fire and slowly raise it to a welding heat, meanwhile turning the stock over and over.

28. When it is molten looking, remove it from the fire and quickly place it on the anvil with the eye extending on the far side and resting even with the edge. Turn the stock until the taper is up and deliver blows until the end is welded down. Continue to hammer around the stock just under the eye until it is perfectly round in section and of the original diameter.

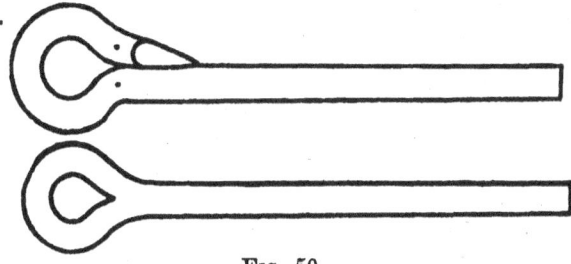

Fig. 50

References:

Bacon, *Forge Practice*, p. 17. Harcourt, *Elementary Forge Practice*, p. 46. Jones, *Forging and Smithing*, p. 82.

Questions:

1. Why upset the stock before making a weld?
2. What should determine the amount a piece of stock should be upset for a weld?
3. What determines the proper length for a scarf?
4. What difficulties arise from having a scarf too long?
5. Why should the end of the scarf be blunt rather than thin?
6. Why should the surface of the scarf be slightly convex rather than concave?
7. Why should all welding heats be taken slowly?
8. Why leave the stock in the fire a few seconds after the blast is shut off before removing to a weld?
9. Why is it necessary to strike the stock on the anvil immediately after removing it from the fire and before welding?
10. Why should very light blows be struck until the pieces are stuck?
11. Why should the end of the scarf be welded down as soon as possible after the weld is started?
12. Why does the difficulty of welding increase with the number of heats?

FORGING TOOL STEEL

Directions:

1. Build a large clean fire and bank the sides and back with damp coal.
2. Place the part of the tool steel that is to be forged in the fire on the bed of coals and cover it with live coals.
3. Turn on a very small amount of blast and raise the heat slowly.
4. If a large piece is being heated, build a large fire and heat the piece very slowly so that the center will reach the forging heat as soon as the outside. When working tool steel it is very important that it be of uniform temperature all the way thru.
5. Never allow steel to soak in the fire with the blast turned off.
6. When the steel reaches a red heat remove it from the fire and forge rapidly to the desired shape.
7. Reheat as often as necessary to keep the steel at a red heat but finish the forging processes with a minimum number of heats.
8. Do not heat tool steel above a bright red heat.

References:

Harcourt, *Elementary Forge Practice*, p. 107. Bacon, *Forge Practice*, p. 197. Ilgen, *Forge Work*, p. 85.

Questions:

1. What is the effect on tool steel of heating it in a low oxidizing fire?
2. Why is it necessary to heat tool steel slowly?
3. What is the effect of forging a piece of tool steel whose outside is hotter than the inside?
4. Why is soaking in the fire with the blast turned off very injurious to tool steel?
5. What is the effect of forging steel at a low temperature?
6. What is the effect of getting steel too hot?

Operation No. 18

ANNEALING TOOL STEEL

Directions:

1. Build a large clean fire—one that is big enough to cover completely the work to be annealed.
2. Place the work to be annealed in the fire on a live bed of coals and cover it to exclude the air of the blast and the room from the steel.
3. Heat very slowly by using only a very small amount of blast until the entire piece is up to a uniform red heat.
4. Remove it from the fire and quickly place it in a box filled with air-slacked lime or pulverized charcoal. Cover it with a heavy layer and allow to remain until cold.
5. If an annealing box is not available and work doesn't require a high degree of accuracy in annealing, heat to a uniform red heat and pack warm dry ashes around the piece on the side of the forge. Leave it until it is entirely cold.

References:

Harcourt, *Elementary Forge Practice*, p. 101. Ilgen *Forge Work*, p. 86.

Questions:

1. Why do we anneal tool steel after it is forged?
2. Why is it necessary to have a uniform heat all the way thru pieces that are being annealed?
3. What is the effect of the cooling of tool steel in air currents?
4. How does the lime affect the steel?
5. Why is lime better than ashes?
6. How are large quantities of steel annealed?
7. What is the probable cause of the annealed piece being uneven in hardness?
8. What is the remedy for such unevenness?

HARDENING TOOL STEEL

Directions:

1. Heat the parts of the work to be hardened in a heavy, clean, non-oxidizing fire to a uniform cherry-red heat known as the "critical temperature."
2. Remove it from the fire and very quickly plunge it into a cooling bath such as cold water, brine, or oil.
3. As the work is cooling keep shifting it in the bath to keep it always surrounded by cool liquid and to prevent the formation of steam pockets on the stock.
4. If many pieces are to be hardened keep the bath cool by adding to it from time to time.

References:

Jones, *Forging and Smithing*, p. 94. Bacon, *Forge Practice*, p. 174.

Questions:

1. Why is it necessary to cool stock quickly in hardening?
2. What is the difference in effect of hardening in oil, brine, and water?
3. Is the critical temperature the same in all grades of tool steel?
4. What is the effect of the formation of steam pockets on the steel?
5. What dangers arise in hardening pieces with holes or pockets in them?
6. What dangers arise in hardening pieces having sharp internal angles or thick and thin parts?

Operation No. 20

TEMPERING TOOL STEEL

Directions:

1. If only a portion of the tool is to be tempered as in the case of a cold chisel, punch, or hammer face, do the hardening and tempering at the same heat.

2. Heat the end of the tool to a cherry-red heat and plunge perpendicularly about an inch of the end in the cooling bath. While the tool is cooling keep moving it around so that it will be surrounded with a cold bath all the time, and up and down thru a short distance to prevent a water crack forming. When the part of the tool in the cooling bath is entirely cold remove it from the bath and polish the hardened surface with an emery cloth to remove all scale.

3. Notice that the heat from the unscaled portion is conducting down toward the end very quickly and that a band of color, straw color, is on one side and blending into blue on the other side, and is forming on the grey hardened surface. Notice that this band of colors is moving toward the end of the stock.

4. Each of the colors in the band represents a different degree of hardness. When the color representing the required degree of hardness for the tool reaches the end plunge the tool until cold. For ordinary cold chisels, for general purposes, cool when the purple reaches the end. For punches and hammer faces, cool when the blue reaches the end.

5. If the tool is to be tempered thruout its length harden and polish the entire tool, then hold the hardened polished tool over the forge fire, bunsen burner, blow torch, or heated piece of iron until the desired color appears. A piece of heated pipe is excellent for small tools. Apply heat all over the hardened surface equally, as it is highly important to have the entire hardened surface change color at the same time. When the desired color appears, plunge the tool quickly until it is cold.

GUIDE FOR HARDENING AND TEMPERING CARBON TOOL STEEL

Applications.	Color of Oxide	Action of File
Engraving tools, lathe tools, and tools for cutting hard metals at slow speed.	Very pale yellow	File will hardly mark
Lathe and planer tools for heavy work, milling cutters, taps, reamers, thread-cutting tools, punches, dies, etc.	Straw yellow	File will mark
Various punches and dies, woodworking tools, twist drills, sledges, blacksmith's hand-hammers, stone drills, etc.	Deep straw (or brown-yellow)	File will mark a little deeper
Shear knives, rivet snaps, punches, boilermakers' tools, and cold chisels for light work.	Light purple	
Cold chisels for ordinary work, gears, surgical instruments, etc.	Blue tinged with red	Files, but with difficulty
Springs, picks, etc.	Blue	
	Grey or green	

6. If the tool breaks or chips when used for the purpose for which it was intended it indicates that it is too hard. Heat the tool very slowly and carefully until it changes to a color representing a slightly lower degree of hardness. For instance, if the tool was cooled when it had a uniform brownish purple color and it chipped or broke under use, it should be heated until the brownish purple color changes to a purple, then cooled.

Operation No. 20
Page No. 3

7. If the tool bends when used for the purpose for which it was intended it indicates that it is too soft. Heat it to a cherry-red heat or critical temperature and plunge to harden. Polish the surface and heat very slowly until the color appears that represents a higher degree of hardness than that at which it was cooled the first time. For instance, if the tool was cooled when the hardened surface had turned to a purple color and it was found that it bent under use, reharden, polish the surface, and heat slowly until the hardened surface changes to a brownish purple color, then cool.

8. In all cases of tempering, test the tool as soon as it is finished.

References:

Jones, *Forging and Smithing*, pp. 97, 141. Harcourt, *Elementary Forge Practice*, p. 103.

Questions:

1. Why polish the surface after the tool is hardened?
2. Why is it advisable in drawing the temper in a small tool to hold it inside a heated pipe instead of over the fire?
3. Why is a water crack likely to form if the stock is not moved up and down during the process of hardening?
4. If the temper is being drawn by the heat remaining in the tool after hardening what will happen if the tool has been cooled too much? If not cooled enough?
5. How will the amount of heat left in the tool affect the width of the band of color?
6. Is there any advantage in having a wide band of color?

WORKING HIGH-SPEED STEEL

Directions:

1. When the forging of high-speed steel is required heat the steel to a high yellow color and quickly forge roughly to shape, at the first heat if possible.
2. Rough-grind it to size and shape the cutting edge.
3. Heat it in a deep, clean, well coked fire until the steel has a white greasy appearance and then plunge it in fish oil and let it remain until it is cold. If no oil is available let it cool in the air. Never plunge high-speed steel in water.
4. Finish the tool by grinding to the required cutting edge.

References:
Jones, *Forging and Smithing*, p. 97.

Operation No. 22

CASE-HARDENING

Directions:

1. For case-hardening work such as wrenches, wrist-pins, etc., use cast-iron box large enough to hold the work. Place a fire brick on each side of the fire-pot of the forge to support the box. Fill the box with potassium cyanide and place it on the bricks. Build a large fire around the box and as the cyanide melts keep adding more until the box is full enough to cover the work.

Caution. Cyanide is very poisonous. Avoid inhaling the fumes or getting particles of it in scratches on the hands.

2. Tie together with small wire the pieces to be hardened so that they may be lifted out of the bath.

3. See that the pieces to be hardened are perfectly dry, then drop them gently into a molten red-hot bath of potassium cyanide. Keep the cyanide hot as long as the work is in it. If the work is to be hardened for a depth of about five thousandths of an inch leave it in the red-hot bath for an hour. For a thicker hardened coat leave it in longer.

4. Remove the work from the cyanide by means of the wire and plunge it in the cooling bath.

5. If mottled brown spots are wanted as a finish on the product use for the cooling bath a solution of saltpeter and water. A handful of saltpeter to two gallons of water gives the proper strength solution.

References:

Bacon, *Forge Practice*, p. 232.

Questions:

1. Why is it necessary to have the work perfectly dry before placing it in red-hot potassium cyanide?
2. Why cool the work quickly after taking from the cyanide?
3. What kind of material may be case-hardened?
4. When is case-hardening desirable?
5. How does the hardness of a case-hardened article compare with the hardness obtained with tool steel?

DRILLING

Directions:

1. Mark the location of the center of the holes to be drilled with a center punch. If great accuracy is required, lay out the exact size of the hole with dividers and make five or six light center-punch marks on this line.

2. Place the work to be drilled on a wooden block or V-block and feed the drill-bit down with the point in the center-punch mark until a spot has been drilled about half the diameter of the hole. Lift the drill and examine the work by means of the center-punch marks to see if the hole is in the exact location desired. If it is necessary to shift the hole use a small gouge-pointed chisel or a center punch and cut a

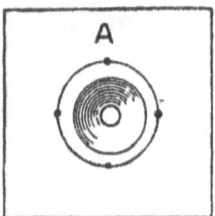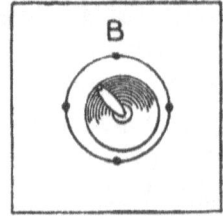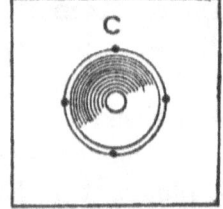

Fig. 51

narrow groove down the side of the spot on the side toward which the hole is to be moved. This groove should be as deep as the distance the drill is off center. A, Fig. 51, shows the drill off center; B shows the groove to make the correction; C shows how it should appear when in the proper position.

3. Turn on the automatic feed and start the drill. Put a small amount of oil on the drill-bit about two inches above the work. Use no oil when drilling cast-iron.

4. Hold the work securely to prevent the stock from spinning around when the drill bit cuts thru the stock.

References:
   Jones, *Forging and Smithing*, p. 32.

Questions:
   1. Why make center-punch marks before starting to drill?
   2. Can you drill tool steel?
   3. What probably is the trouble if the drill fails to cut?
   4. What is the trouble if the drill throws out chips on one side only in drilling soft steel?
   5. When is it desirable to drill rather than punch a hole?
   6. Why will a small groove on the side of the spot when the drill is started draw the drill in that direction?

TAPPING

Directions:

1. Drill holes for tapping U. S. S. threads according to the sizes given in the table below:

Diam. Tap in Inches	Threads Per Inch	Size of Drill
1/4	20	3/16
5/16	18	1/4
3/8	16	5/16
7/16	14	3/8
1/2	13	13/32
1/2	12	13/32
9/16	12	29/64
5/8	11	33/64
11/16	11	37/64
3/4	10	5/8
13/16	10	11/16
7/8	9	47/64
15/16	9	51/64
1	8	27/32
1 1/8	7	61/64

If the size for the tap drill is indicated on the tap, use that size in preference to the size given in the table.

2. Select a taper tap the required size and clamp it securely in the tap wrench. If one end of the hole is closed and threads must be cut to the bottom of the hole use a plug tap first then a bottoming tap. If the depth of the hole will permit it use a taper tap first then a plug tap, then a bottoming tap.

3. Grasp the wrench directly over the tap with one hand and place the tap in the hole, being careful that it is in line with the hole. Press the tap firmly into the hole and turn it to the right. Continue to turn as long as the tap can be turned with one hand.

4. Oil the tap freely then grasp the handles of the tap wrench with both hands. With a firm, steady movement continue to turn the wrench, turning backward slightly every two turns, until the tap is thru the hole.

5. Be careful not to try to turn the tap after the bottom of the hole is reached.

References:
Jones, *Forging and Smithing*, p. 34.

Questions:
1. Why start the tap with one hand placed directly over the tap?
2. Why use care to see that the tap is in line with the hole?
3. Why use the taper tap first?
4. How do you secure a full thread when using a taper tap?
5. Why use oil on the tap?
6. Why turn the tap backward slightly every second turn?

CUTTING THREADS

Directions:

1. Point slightly with a file the rod or bolt to be threaded and clamp securely in the vise.

2. Choose a die the required size, fasten it in the stock, and place it over the end of the work where threads are to be cut.

3. Grasp the stock close up to the die, press firmly against the work and at the same time turn to the right, being sure to keep the die straight on the work.

4. Oil the end of the work and continue to turn the stock rocking it backward slightly every two revolutions until the thread is cut the required length.

5. Remove the die by turning it to the left.

6. If left hand threads are to be cut use a left hand die and turn the die to the left.

References:

Jones, *Forging and Smithing*, p. 37.

Questions:

1. Why point the end of the rod or bolt slightly before cutting thread?
2. Why hold the stock near the die rather than by the handles while starting?
3. Why rock the die backward slightly every two revolutions while cutting threads?
4. Why apply oil while cutting threads?

BENDING PIPE

Directions:

1. When bending a piece of pipe it tends to collapse in the direction of the bend and spread in the opposite direction. Since it cannot collapse unless it is permitted to spread, any means that will prevent its spreading will prevent its collapse.

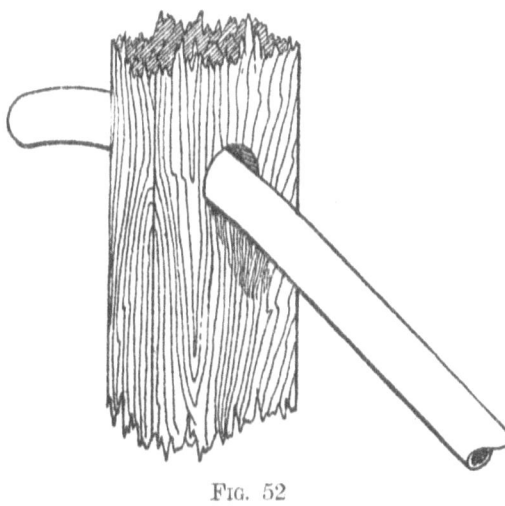

Fig. 52

2. Where only a few pieces of small pipe are to be bent they should be clamped lightly in a vise or clamp, at the point where the bend is to be made, to prevent the spreading of the sides, and bend the pipe in the direction of the opening of the jaws.

The seam of the pipe should be on the inside of the bend slightly to one side of the center

3. A very effective and convenient method is to fasten up a heavy board or plank and bore a hole in it about ¼″ larger in diameter than the pipe. Slip the pipe thru the hole and bend slightly Shift the pipe forward or backward as the bending is continued in order to secure the desired curve. Fig. 52. Fig. 53 shows another pipe bending device.

4. A hickey may be used to bend small pipe by placing the hickey on the pipe where the curve is to begin, stand on the pipe and pull on the handle of the hickey until the pipe bends slightly, then move the hickey a little farther on the curve and

bend again. Continue this until the desired curve is obtained. Fig. 54.

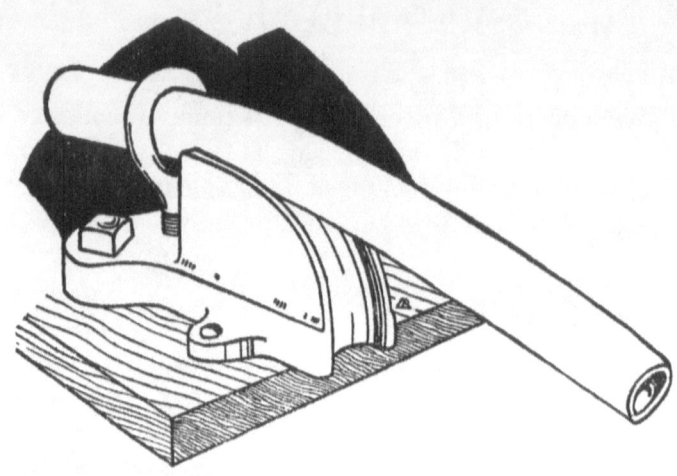

Fig. 53

5. Bend a large pipe by placing a cap on the end and heating to an even red heat where the bend is to be made, and while one end is supported on some object drop the other end on the ground or floor

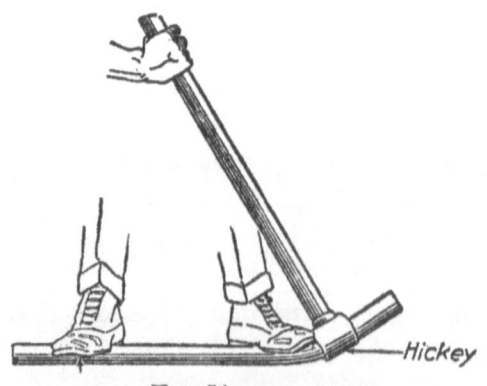

Fig. 54

References:
Bacon, *Forge Practice*, p. 226.

RIVETING

Directions:

1. Press together firmly the pieces to be riveted and select a rivet large enough to fit the hole snugly, and long enough to extend thru the hole for heading a distance equal to the diameter of the rivet. If the rivet is too long cut it off with the nippers and square it with a file.

2. Put the rivet in the rivet hole and rest the head on the solid portion of the anvil. Hold the pieces firmly together and strike medium heavy blows in the center of the end of the rivet with the peen of the ball-peen hammer Then, with the face of the hammer strike squarely on the end of the rivet until the pieces being riveted are fastened firmly together, and the end of the rivet extends above the pieces one-half its original distance.

3. Raise the handle of the hammer and strike around the circumference of the end of the rivet at an angle of 45 degrees until an oval top is formed, the edge of which fits snugly against the stock being riveted.

4. Finish by striking a medium heavy blow directly on top of the rivet.

5. Finish the rivet top with a rivet set if one is available.

6. If the work is of such character that it cannot be placed on the anvil hold a heavy sledge against the rivet head while riveting.

7. If a straight rivet is being used where the head is to be formed on both ends use a rivet that is long enough to extend on each side approximately the diameter of the rivet.

8. Place the rivet thru the holes, press the pieces firmly together, and set the rivet on end on the face of the anvil with the pieces to be riveted half way between the top and bottom of the rivet. In this position strike a heavy blow on the end of the rivet with the peen of ball-peen hammer then turn the work over and strike the other end of the rivet in like manner

Then strike the ends of the rivet alternately with the face of the hammer until the ends stick out from the work a distance equal to half the diameter of the rivet. Then finish with a rivet set or by striking around the end at an angle of 45 degrees.

9. If two pieces are to be riveted together that must move with reference to each other, as in the case of shears, etc., place a piece of paper between the members before riveting.

10. In all cases of riveting, the work may be done with greater ease if the rivets are first heated.

References:

Jones, *Forging and Smithing*, p. 77

Questions:

1. What is the effect of having the rivet extend thru the pieces too far? Not far enough?
2. What is the effect of having the rivet too small?
3. Why should the pieces being riveted be held firmly together?
4. Why strike in the center of the rivet with the ball of the ball-peen hammer first?
5. Why use a rivet set for finishing the head?
6. When the rivet is cut, why finish or square the end with a file before heating?
7. Why put paper between the members when the parts are to move with reference to each other?
8. What determines the thickness of the paper being used?

Operation No. 28 69

REMOVING BROKEN STUD BOLT

Directions:

1. If the stud bolt extends above the surface, flatten the sides so that an ordinary wrench may be used or use a pipe wrench to screw it out.

2. If the stud seems very tight when the pressure of the wrench is on it strike the end of the stud with the hammer while trying to screw it out.

3. If the stud is broken off even with the surface make a center-punch mark in the end and drill a hole in it about one inch deep and about half the diameter of the stud.

4. Choose an "Ezy Out" with a twist in the opposite direction to the direction of the threads and one whose diameter is slightly smaller than the hole and start it into the hole. Put a wrench or handle on the "Ezy Out" and with slow steady pressure turn in the direction that will unscrew the stud. Fig. 55.

5. If an "Ezy Out" is not available, drive a piece of tempered steel tapered to a square into the hole until the corners are imbedded in the side of the hole. Use a wrench on the steel to take the stud out.

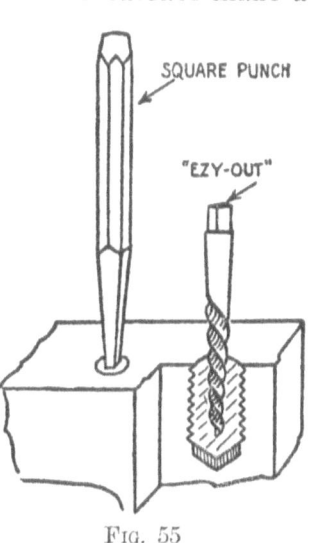

Fig. 55

6. If the stud is still stuck fast, drill a hole exactly in the middle of the stud large enough so that only a thin rim of the stud is left. With a small fine pointed chisel pry out the rim of the stud.

7 If the stud is rusted tightly in the hole apply heat until the expansion of the material breaks the rust, then twist the stud out.

8. If the projecting stud is to be removed without injury to the thread on the projecting end, screw on a nut until the stud projects thru the nut a little more than its thickness. Screw on a second nut until it is tight against the first as a lock nut. Apply a wrench to the first nut and unscrew the stud.

References:

Jones, *Forging and Smithing*, p. 165.

Questions:

1. What are the reasons for studs breaking off?
2. What is the action on the stud when a tapered square is driven into the hole?
3. What is the effect when the stud is struck while trying to twist it out?
4. Why center-punch the end of the stud before drilling?

Operation No. 29

SAWING WITH HACK-SAW

Directions:

1. To fit a hack-saw blade in a frame, grasp the hack-saw frame near the middle with the left hand. Attach the blade at the end of the frame opposite the handle so that the teeth of the saw point away from the handle. Adjust the frame to the length of the blade and fasten the blade in the handle end. Screw the handle to the right or tighten the wing nut to the other end of the frame until the blade is perfectly tight and will not buckle.

2. If loose work is to be sawed clamp it securely in the vise.

3. To saw thin work or tubing use a blade with fine teeth, about 24 teeth to the inch. For general purposes use a blade with about 16 or 18 teeth to the inch.

4. Grasp the handle of the hack-saw with the right hand, the left hand holding the opposite end of the frame. Fig. 56.

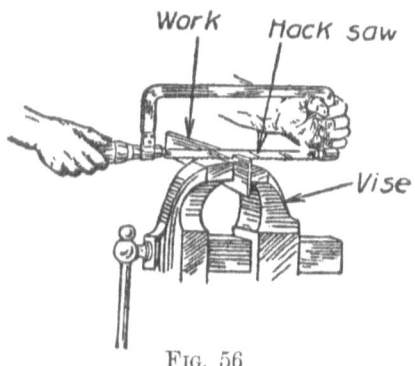

Fig. 56

5. Start the cut by applying light steady pressure on the forward stroke and relieving it on the return stroke. In starting out with new blades use extreme care in making the first few strokes.

6. Use long steady strokes, applying slight pressure on the forward stroke and releasing on the backward stroke until the cut is finished. Make about forty strokes per minute.

7. In starting a cut on a sharp corner notch the work with a file or cold chisel enough so that at least two teeth will engage.

8. In sawing very thin stock place it in a vise between two pieces of wood and saw thru the wood and metal at the same time.

9. In sawing thin stock incline the handle of the saw so that as many teeth as possible will be engaged at one time.

10. When finishing a cut raise the handle of the saw slightly so as to avoid the teeth catching on the thin, sharp edge of the stock.

Questions:

1. Why is it important to have the correct tension on the blade while sawing?
2. Why should a fine-toothed blade be used on tubing and thin work?
3. Why use special care in starting new blades?
4. Why start the cut on a sharp corner with a file or cold chisel?
5. Why hold the saw frame with both hands?
6. Why apply pressure on the forward and release on the backward stroke? What is the effect of too heavy pressure?
7. What is the cause of the saw binding?
8. Why should the work be held securely?
9. Why place thin stock between pieces of wood for sawing?
10. What is the result of the teeth catching on the thin, sharp edge of the stock when finishing the cut?

Operation No. 30 73

SOLDERING

Directions:

1. Tin the soldering copper as follows. Heat the point and brighten it with a file. Re-heat until it will melt the solder freely and rub the point of the copper on a lump of sal-ammoniac to clean it. Melt a few drops of solder on the sal-ammoniac and rub the copper in it until the solder sticks to the copper A little powdered rosin on a brick or board will do instead of sal-ammoniac.

2. Keep the copper clean by occasionally dipping it quickly while hot in a solution of sal-ammoniac. Make a solution by mixing one part sal-ammoniac with twenty parts water

3. Place the pieces of metal in position ready for soldering and fasten them so they will not become displaced while soldering. If it is old work scrape the seam clean.

4. Apply to the seam a flux suited to the work as follows:
    For galvanized iron, use raw muriatic acid.

Fig. 57

For copper, brass, zinc and iron use cut acid or chloride of zinc.

Cut acid is muriatic acid in which has been placed all the small pieces of zinc it will dissolve.

For bright tin use powdered rosin.

Specially prepared fluxes may be used for purposes recommended by manufacturers.

5. Heat the soldering copper until it will melt solder freely but it must not be hot enough to burn off the tinning. Hold the hot copper about three inches from your cheek for an instant and note the heat. With a little practice this will enable one to judge the proper heat.

6. With the hot copper tack the seam together at several points with drops of solder, Fig. 57, so as to hold the parts in proper position while soldering.

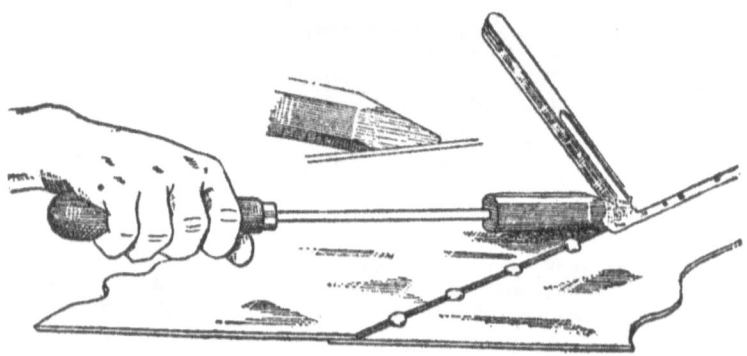

FIG. 58

7 Place the point of the hot, tinned soldering copper on the edge of the seam and touch the copper with a bar of solder Move the copper slowly along the seam for a short distance. As the copper melts the solder, deposit a small quantity along the edge of the seam. Move the copper back to the starting point and hold one of the flat sides of the copper on the seam until the metal becomes as hot as the melted solder then move the copper along the seam slowly enough to remelt the solder deposited along the edge and permit it to flow in between the laps of the seam. Do not move the

copper back and forth and do not use too much solder Fig. 58.

8. When changing or reheating the copper, hold the hot one at the point where you left off, long enough to remelt the solder under the seam.

9. To sweat pieces together apply flux, and tin with solder the surfaces to be joined. Place the tinned surfaces together and heat with torch or soldering copper until the solder melts. Hold the pieces together until the solder cools.

References:

Jones, *Forging and Smithing*, p. 85.

Questions:

1. Of what metal is the soldering copper made?
2. Why should it be heated before brightening or tinning?
3. Why should the soldering copper be tinned?
4. Why is sal-ammoniac or rosin used in tinning the soldering copper?
5. What will be the effect if the soldering copper gets too hot?
6. Why must surfaces to be soldered be bright and clean?
7. Why not heat the soldering copper red hot after it has been tinned?
8. What is the purpose of a flux?
9. Why should soldering coppers be cleaned before soldering?
10. Why is the soldering copper drawn flat and slowly over the seam while soldering?
11. Why must you move the iron more slowly over thick metal than thin metal?
12. What makes the solder stick?

BRAZING

Directions:

1. Brighten with an emery cloth or with a file the parts to be brazed.
2. Fasten the parts together so the joint fits snugly and so they will remain in position while brazing.
3. Direct the torch flame on the joint until the metal becomes a dark red.
4. Apply powdered borax to the seam and return to the flame until the borax melts.
5. Remove the work from the flame and apply a small amount of spelter over the seam. Hold it in the flame again until the spelter melts and runs thru the seam, then remove it from the flame, and with a piece of metal wipe from the surface the surplus spelter before it hardens. When cold smooth the seam with a file.

References:

Bacon, *Forge Practice*, p. 222.

Questions:

1. Why is it necessary to brighten the parts to be brazed?
2. Why should the metal be heated to a red heat before applying borax or spelter?
3. Why is borax used?
4. What is spelter?
5. What material is sometimes used instead of spelter?
6. Why must spelter melt at a lower temperature than the metal being brazed?

Operation No. 32

BABBITTING AND SCRAPING BEARINGS

Directions.

1. Clean thoroly the box to be babbitted and be sure that no moisture is left on the surface.

2. Select a babbitting mandrel for the job to be done. In many jobs the regular shaft or journal must be used, but use a special mandrel when possible. If the bearing is to be bored and reamed use a mandrel slightly smaller than the shaft.

3. Cover the babbitting mandrel with a coating of graphite mixed with gasoline, wrap a piece of thin paper around it, or smoke it with a candle if babbitting a solid bearing.

4. Have the bearing shell in a vertical position whenever possible.

5. Put the babbitting mandrel in place and line it up so that the shaft will be in its required position with reference to the bearing shell. In the case of a crank shaft place the mandrel equidistant from the bearing shell on all sides for the two end bearings. Then place the shaft in position in these two bearings and pour the others so that they will be in line.

6. Fill all oil holes with asbestos. In cases where the bearing must be poured thru oil holes leave the most convenient one open.

7 Make joints tight with putty. If there is a space of a quarter inch or more, wooden or cardboard heads should be cut to fit the mandrel and clamped in place or backed up with putty In all cases ample vents must be left for the escape of air and gases while the bearing is being poured.

8. Make a funnel of putty around the hole thru which the metal is to be poured.

9. Secure more than enough babbitt of the required grade, put it in a cast-iron pot or ladle, and place it over a forge fire or gas burner When the metal is molten cover it with powdered coal or dust. The babbitt is ready to pour when it will char a freshly whittled pine stick brown in three or four

seconds. If the stick trembles in the fingers and smoke rises, the metal is too hot. Care should be taken not to allow this condition to occur

10. When possible heat the bearing box and mandrel until it is quite hot to the touch before pouring the bearing.

11. When everything is in readiness to pour, sprinkle a little powdered rosin on the surface of the babbitt and stir. With a warm ladle dip from the bottom of the pot. Bring the ladle up quickly so as to force back the dirt on top of the pot. If the babbitt is melted in the ladle that is to be used for pouring, do not skim off the top but use a helper to hold back the scum as the metal is being poured. Pour the metal into the bearing in a clean steady stream as large as the opening will allow Never falter or hesitate during the pouring operation since the bearing must be filled by a continuous stream of metal. On a large bearing use two ladles if possible and pour from opposite corners of the bearing.

12. When the babbitt has hardened, remove the fixtures and the mandrel and take out the plugs from the oil holes.

13. In cases where the bearing is to be in halves, place a cardboard shim between the halves and let it extend over to the mandrel or the shaft. Cut a V-shaped hole in the cardboard next to the mandrel or shaft so that the metal may reach and fill the under half Holes must not be cut larger than a quarter of an inch even for large bearings.

14. File the surfaces of each half smooth, and level the corners. Remove the fins or burs with a draw-knife or file. Any holes filled with a babbitt may be cleaned out with a hot iron.

15. If shrinkage occurs, peen the babbitt to tighten it by hammering lightly along the center of the bearing with the round end of a ball-peen hammer Extend the blows on either side of the center line until babbitt is tight.

16. Place the halves of bearing together, with the shim between, screw down tight and ream or bore to approximately the size of the shaft.

17. Place the shaft in the bearing, screw the cap down in place. Turn the shaft a few turns, remove the cap and note

where shaft rubbed on the bearing. Scrape these high places down with the bearing scraper. Coat the shaft with Prussian blue and replace in bearing. Turn in the bearing several times, remove it and with a bearing scraper, scrape off the blue spots left on the bearing. Continue this process until the shaft will leave seventy-five per cent of the bearing surface blue when turned in it. See Figs. 59 and 60.

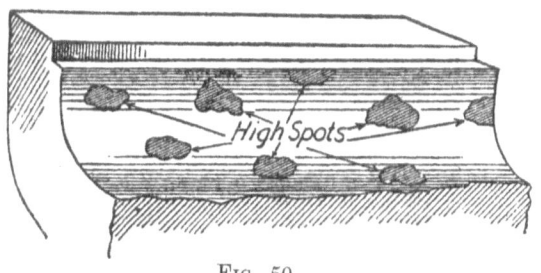

FIG. 59

18. Where oil holes are to be small, and have not been preserved by the use of a plug, drill new oil holes.

19. With a curved grooving chisel cut oil grooves from a point near each corner of the bearing to the oil hole.

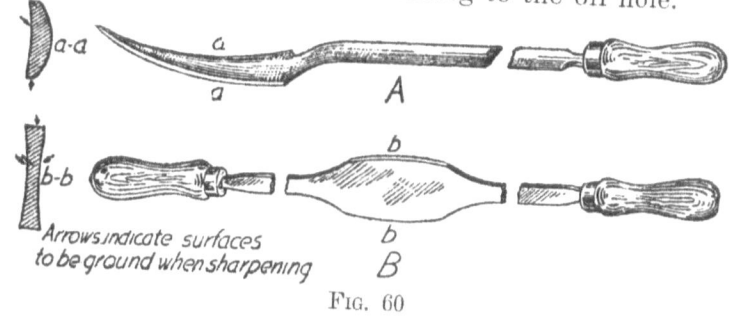

FIG. 60

References:

Jones, *Forging and Smithing*, p. 159.

Questions:

1. Why should the bearing box be heated before the metal is poured in?
2. What is the advantage of having large mandrels hollow?
3. Why should babbitting mandrels be slightly tapered?
4. Why should more than enough babbitt metal be melted?
5. Why should the babbitting mandrel be coated with graphite and gasoline or smoke before using?
6. Why is it necessary to have the bearing shell perfectly dry before pouring in the hot metal?
7 Why put powdered rosin on molten metal before pouring?
8. Why should a large bearing be poured from both sides?

FILING

Directions

1. Clamp the work firmly in the vise with the surface to be filed in a horizontal position.

2. If much material is to be removed use a flat bastard cut file and finish with a double-cut second-cut file. The size of the work will determine the size of the file used.

3. Grasp the handle of the file with the right hand and hold the end between the thumb and fingers of the left hand. Fig. 61. When using a large file for making heavy cuts, place the weight of the hand on the end of the file.

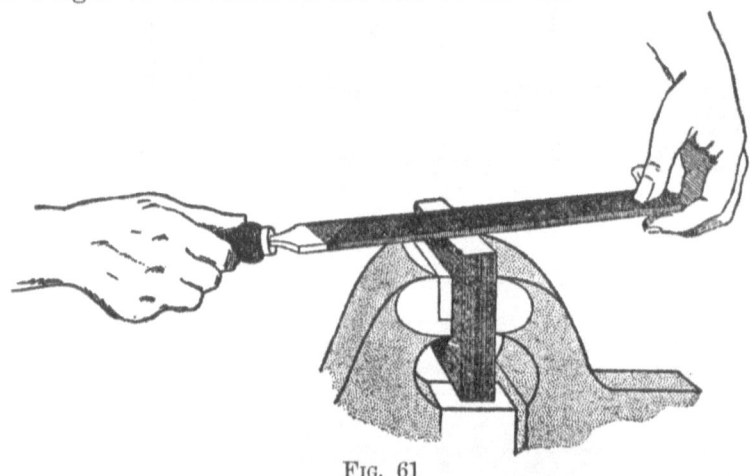

FIG. 61.

4. Hold the file firmly and push it in a straight line across the work, being careful that the pressure is uniform and that the front end of the file does not dip near the end of the stroke. If a curved surface is being filed push the file in such a way that it follows the curve of the work.

5. Release the pressure on the backward stroke of the file.

6. If the surface being filed tends to become high in the center, place the end of the file about the center of the high place, elevate the handle slightly, apply pressure on the file

Operation No. 33
Page No. 2

over the high place, and use very short strokes until the high place is filed out. Then use long straight strokes to smooth the surface.

FIG. 62

7 For smoothing long narrow surfaces grasp the file by the ends, place it crosswise on the surface, and draw it back and forth over the work. This is called draw filing. Fig. 62.

8. If the file tends to pull out small pieces of metal, leaving a rough surface, chalk the surface of the file freely before using it.

Questions:

1. What is the difference between a double-cut bastard and a double-cut second-cut file?
2. Why should a file be pushed in a straight line when filing a plane surface?
3. Why are general purpose files manufactured with bulged sides?
4. Why release the pressure on the backstroke of a file?

HOW TO SHARPEN A SAW

Directions

To Sharpen a Rip-Saw:

1. Arrange a saw vise or clamp so the best light to be secured will shine on the side of the saw next to the operator and so the top of the vise will be at a level nearly with the height of the arm pits.

2. Examine the saw teeth for evenness of length by sighting down the rows of teeth, and also for depth of gullets. A gullet should never be less than one-half, nor more than all of the distance between the points. For slow cutting in hard wood a shallow gullet is required and for fast cutting, a deep gullet. For general purposes make the depth of the gullet three-fourths the distance between points.

3. If all the teeth are not of the same length, top-joint them as follows:
    a   Clamp the saw in a vise so that its teeth extend 2 or 3 inches above the vise jaws.
    (b Hold a 10 or 12-inch flat mill file, tang toward you, in both hands so the extended thumbs will lie together along the top side of the file, and the closed fingers will form a guide on each side of the saw blade.
    c   Begin at the handle end of the saw, and with the file held level, run it over the teeth the entire length of the blade until all the teeth are made the same length. Note: Files do not cut on return strokes.

4. If the saw is in bad condition do not continue to top-joint until all the teeth are of the same length, but joint off one-fourth the length of all the longer teeth, then file them to an approximate shape and top-joint again.

5. Secure a saw-set and adjust it so as to give only enough set to the teeth to allow the blade to slip readily thru the wood; and measuring from the top of a tooth, make the bend for the set not more than one-half the length of the tooth.

6. To set the rip-saw, rest the end of the blade, tooth edge up, against some solid object, as a bench top, and hold along the back of the blade with the left hand, so that the handle will rest against the body Bend every other tooth outward, then turn the saw around and bend the remaining teeth in the opposite direction.

7 To file the rip-saw use a 5" slim taper, triangular file for saws with eight or more points to inch, and a 6" file for seven or less.

8. Clamp the saw in a saw vise so that its handle end is to the left and the teeth are not more than ¼" above the saw-vise jaws.

9. Grasp the handle of the file in the right hand, the thumb on top, and the point in the left hand, between the thumb and forefinger, the thumb on top.

10. Beginning at the handle end of the saw, place the file between two of the teeth so that its left side will be in contact with the first tooth that slants away from the worker.

11. Hold the file level and at right angles to the saw blade. *Keep its left side in a vertical position.*

12. *Run the file its full length* across the teeth, maintaining a uniform movement and slight pressure on the forward stroke only Relieve all weight on return strokes; do not drag the file.

13. Hold your hands so that every stroke will be made in the same direction.

14. File all teeth that point away from the worker, taking not more than three strokes across each tooth and skipping all low teeth until the high teeth are cut level with the low.

15. Run the saw handle end to the right, and file the remaining teeth.

16. When taking the second or third stroke of the file, sight to see that its left side is in contact with all of the front side of the left tooth and the right side in contact with all of the back side of the right tooth.

17 File all the teeth so that the front side is vertical and all the gullets of the same depth. If some of the teeth are

of uneven size, crowd the file against the larger tooth and bear lightly against the smaller, until all are of the same size.

18. Side joint the teeth by laying the saw blade on a flat board and run a fine mill file or an oilstone lightly along the side of the blade and teeth, then turn the saw over and joint the other side.

To Sharpen Crosscut-Saw

1. Read carefully the directions for sharpening a rip-saw.
2. Top-joint, then set by bending every other tooth toward its point.
3. To file, begin at the handle end place the file between two of the teeth; slant its top side slightly toward the tooth in front; point its end in the direction of the small end of the saw so that it forms an angle of 45 degrees with the side of the saw; then file from one side all teeth that point away from the worker
4. Turn the saw and file the remaining teeth, then side joint.

References:

Griffith, *Essentials of Woodworking*, pp. 27-28. Noyes, *Handwork in Wood*, pp. 67-68.

Questions:
1. Why side joint the teeth?
2. Why file stubby teeth before setting?
3. Why hold the file always at the same angle?
4. Why set a saw?
5. Why not set all saws alike?
6. What will be the effect of side jointing only one side of a saw?
7 If the saw always tends to leave the line in the same direction, what are the probable causes?
8. Why are the teeth of a rip-saw always filed at right angles to the blade?
9. Why must all teeth of a saw be of the same length?
10. Why must all teeth of a saw be filed at the same angle?
11. Why must all gullets of a saw be of the same depth?

SETTING WAGON TIRE

Directions

1. Remove the wheel from the wagon and lay it on the ground, the point of the hub down.
2. Make a cold-chisel mark on the edge of the tire and extend it across on the felloe.
3. If two front or two rear tires are to be set at the same time, mark one of them with one mark and the other with two marks.
4. Stand the wheel on edge with the point of the hub to the left, and remove the tire by striking on the right side of the felloe just under the tire. Continue around the rim until the tire is free.
5. If the tire refuses to slip, even tho it is apparently loose, it is probably being held on by short iron pins driven thru the tire. Locate the pins by driving a thin chisel between the tire and the felloe and looking thru the crack. Place a large sledge against the edge of the tire at the place where the pin is and cut the pin off by driving a very thin cold chisel between the felloe and the tire.
6. When the tire is free from the felloe, remove the cut pins from the tire and the felloe and examine the wheels for loose spokes and broken felloes.
7. Renew the felloes if any broken or split ones are found, and tighten the spokes in the felloes by driving hickory wedges, crosswise of the rim, in the end of the spoke tenons. First split the spoke tenon with a thin chisel, start the wedge, then strike alternately on the wedge and the felloe until the spoke is tight.
8. If the rim tends to become rim bound during the process of wedging, make a saw cut between the ends of the felloes at one joint as the wedging proceeds.
9. When all the spokes are wedged, run a saw thru between the ends of the felloes at one joint until they slide loosely

past each other   Redowel the joint between the felloes where it has been cut with the saw

10. Place the wheel on the trestle, the point of the hub down. Drive a small block of wood between two spokes that have an opening in the rim between them and wedge until all the opening in the rim is between these two spokes.

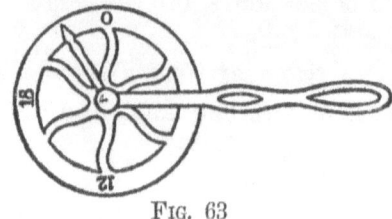

Fig. 63

11. Grasp the tire measuring wheel (Fig. 63) by the handle and place zero graduation mark of the measuring wheel even with the right hand side of the opening between the ends of the felloes. Walk around the wheel to the right, letting the tire measuring wheel travel on the outside of the rim, near the center. Fig. 64. Go clear around the wheel and when the tire measuring wheel crosses the opening, stop and set the pointer on the wheel even with the left side of the opening between the ends of the felloes.

Fig. 64

12. Place the tire down over your head with one edge resting on the anvil and the other on the forge. Make a pencil mark across the tire on the inside. Set the zero graduation mark of the measuring wheel even with this mark and travel

Operation No. 35
Page No. 3

to the right around the tire. Proceed until the pencil mark is reached. The distance the pointer lacks in coming up even with the mark, or the distance to the left of the mark is the amount the tire is larger than the rim. If the tire is the same size as the rim the pointer will come even with the mark. If the pointer falls to the right of the mark the tire is smaller than the rim. When shrunk, the tire should be from $1/8''$ to $5/16''$ smaller than the rim in order to give a draw

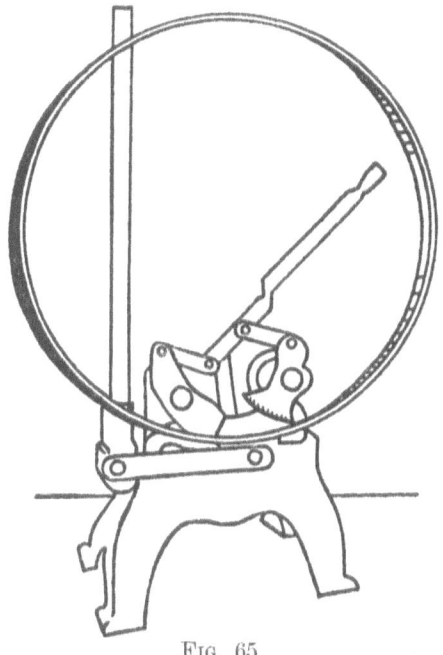

Fig. 65

13. Heat the tire and place it in the tire shrinker. Fig. 65. Clamp and shrink, meanwhile hammering down any kinks that may be forming. Remove from the shrinker, place on the anvil, first on the edge then flatwise, hammering as you do so, until the tire is smooth. Run or measure the tire to see if it has enough draw Repeat these operations until the pointer of the tire measuring wheel falls from $1/8''$ to $5/16''$ to the right of the pencil mark. The amount of the draw will depend upon the thickness of the tire and the condition

of the wheel. Very old, loose wheels may require as much as a ⅜" draw. If a very accurate job is required, cool the tire before measuring.

14. Place the tire upright in the large forge fire, supporting it on bricks placed on each side of the fire pot. Have a chisel mark on the tire next to the chimney Heat to a red heat, then turn the tire in the fire about a foot, and heat again. Continue to heat and turn until the tire is hot all the way around. Turn the tire down so it lies flat on the forge, grasp it with tongs to the left of the chisel mark. Place the tire on the rim so that the chisel mark on the tire and the mark on the felloe coincide. With a tire puller (Fig. 66) or a wide-jawed pair of tongs in the left hand and a hammer in the right, force the tire down over the rim by clamping over the top edge of the tire and under the edge of the rim and

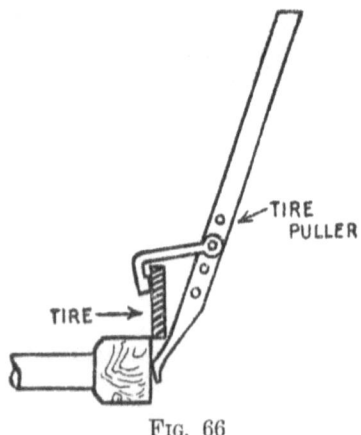

Fig. 66

striking the inside edge of the tire with the hammer at an angle of 45 degrees.

15. When the tire is in place and as the cooling proceeds, remove the wheel to the slack tub and hammer over the ends of the spokes. Have a helper turn the wheel in the slack tub and with a hand hammer in each hand even up the tire on the rim by holding one hammer against the tire and striking the rim on the opposite side. To take out irregularities in a curva-

Operation No. 35
Page No. 5

ture, continue to strike on the ends of the spokes until the tire is cold.

16. If more than one wagon tire is to be set, shrink all the tires to the required size and then stack them on four bricks in the shop yard with all the chisel marks together and on the top side. Stack around them finely split dry wood or bark and start a fire. Arrange the wheels in the order for receiving the tires and place the first wheel on trestles. When the fire dies down sufficiently draw out one tire with a hook or tongs and place on the wheel. If the tire is very hot and is burning the rim pour water on before removing from the trestles.

References:

Jones, *Forging and Smithing*, p. 173.

Questions:

1. Why is the tire taken off towards the inside of the wheel rather than the outside?
2. Why is it a bad practice to drive pins that extend only part way thru a felloe thru the tire to hold it on?
3. What is the effect of too much draw?
4. How can you prevent excessive dishing and still draw a wheel perfectly tight?
5. Why mark the tire and rim before the tire is removed?
6. When working on wheels of approximately the same size, why place different marks on the wheels?
7 Why put in wedges crosswise of the felloe?
8. In wedging spokes why strike alternately on the wedge and felloc?
9. Why put dowels in the ends of felloes?
10. Why should a tire be replaced on a wheel in the same relative position as when it was removed?

SETTING BUGGY TIRE

Directions.

1. Unscrew the nuts and drive out the bolts as far as they can be conveniently driven with a hammer and remove with a large pair of end pinchers. Place the wheel on a bench-wheel rack, (Fig. 67) the point of the hub up; and clamp securely With a file or cold chisel make a shallow mark near one of the joints of the rim.

2. Set the wheel on edge, point the hub to the left, and remove the tire by striking the rim on the side just under the tire. If the tire is rather tight, turn the wheel so that the tire slips the same amount all the way around. Continue until the tire is free from the rim.

3. Replace on the wheel rack, screw down, and examine the rim for splits and ends of spokes for wear or broken tenons. Examine at the hub to see if spokes are loose. If the rim does not fit closely on the ends of the spokes, the wheel is rim bound.

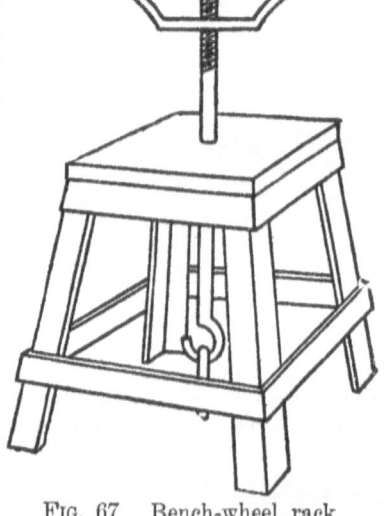

FIG. 67   Bench-wheel rack.

4. If the wheel is rim bound, saw a very small amount off one end of one of the half rims. Split the ends of the tenons of the spokes crosswise of the rim with a thin chisel, and wedge with hickory wedges. Start a wedge in the end of the spoke, then hit the rim at the side of the wedge. Continue to strike alternately the rim and the wedge until the rim fits down snugly on the shoulder of the spoke. Continue around the rim until all the spokes are wedged. If during the wedging process the ends of the rim come together, and the wheel

Operation No. 36
Page No. 2

is rim bound again saw out a small amount at the opening. Usually a saw cut thru an opening between rim halves is sufficient. Continue to saw and wedge until the halves slide loosely past each other

5. Remove the wheel from the wheel rack and place on trestles, the point of the hub down.

6. If the wheel is loose in the hub and has too much dish, saw out more of the rim, usually from 1/16" to 1/8", the amount depending upon how much you think the spokes can be driven into the hub. Place on a wheel rack (Fig. 68) so that the wheel may be screwed down to prevent too much dishing. Screw down until pressure is on the hub and the rim is resting firmly on the frame.

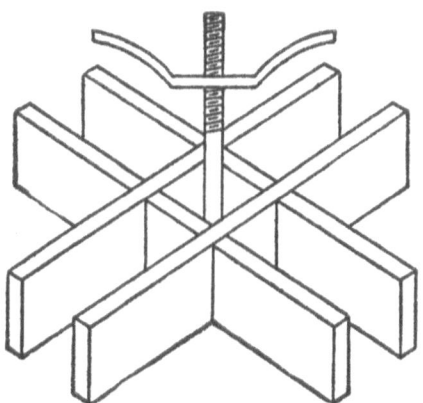

Fig. 68. Rack for fastening down wheel to prevent too much dish.

7 Drive a small block of wood between the two spokes that come on either side of one of the openings in the rim. Wedge down until all the opening in the rim is at one place.

8. Grasp a tire measuring wheel by the handle and place the zero graduation mark of the measuring wheel at the right hand side of the opening between the ends of the rim. Walk around the wheel to the right, letting the wheel travel on the outside of the rim. Go clear around the wheel and when the tire measuring wheel crosses the opening, stop and set the pointer on the wheel even with the left side of the opening.

9. Place the tire down over your head with one edge resting on the anvil and the other on the forge. Make a pencil mark across the tire on the inside. Set the zero graduation mark of the measuring wheel even with this mark and travel to the right around the tire. Proceed until the pencil mark is reached. The distance the pointer lacks in coming even with the mark, or the distance to the left of the mark, is the amount the tire is larger than the rim. If the tire is the same size as the rim the pointer will come even with the mark. If the pointer falls to the right of the mark the tire is smaller than the rim. When shrunk, the tire should be from 1/16″ to 1/8″ smaller than the rim in order to give a draw

10. Heat the tire and place t in the tire shrinker Clamp and shrink, meanwhile hammering down any kinks that may be forming. Remove the tire from the shrinker and place it on the anvil, first on the edge and then flatwise, and hammer until the tire is smooth. Run or measure the tire to see if it has enough draw Repeat these operations until the pointer of the tire measuring wheel falls from 1/16″ to 1/8″ to the right of the pencil mark on the tire, depending on the condition of the wheel. If a very accurate job is required cool the tire before measuring.

11. Place the tire in a forge fire with a mark on the edge next to the chimney of the forge, the tire standing straight up. Heat until it is red hot. Turn the tire in the fire for about a foot and heat again until it is red hot. Continue to turn and heat until the tire is hot all the way around. Turn the tire down so it lies flat on the forge, grasp it with tongs to the right of the file mark, take the tire bolt in the right hand, and proceed to the wheel. Place the tire on the rim so that the file mark on the rim and the file mark on the tire coincide, and slip the bolt thru the hole. With a tire puller or wide-jawed pair of tongs in the left hand and a hammer in the right hand, force the tire down over the rim by clamping over the top edge of the tire and striking with the hammer at an angle of about 45 degrees.

12. When the tire is in place, hammer over the end of the

spokes. If the wheel is not screwed down, remove to the slack tub, place upright on the edge and turn thru water until the tire is cold, meanwhile evening up the tire on the rim by striking over the ends of the spokes. Hammer down any irregularities in the curvature of the tire until it fits the rim snugly.

13. If the wheel is screwed down on the wheel rack, pour water on the rim until cold, meanwhile hammering over the ends of the spokes to drive tightly into the hub. Even up the tire on the rim by holding the heavy hammer on the tire and striking on the rim with another hammer If the draw of the tire tends to dish the wheel rather than pull the spokes into the hub, screw down as the tire cools.

14. Replace the wheel on the bench wheel rack, screw down and use a wood drill and brace to open up the bolt holes. Put in bolts.

15. If the wheel is rather loose in the hub, place it on the anvil, the point of the hub up so that the head of the hub rivets are resting on the edge of the anvil. In this position place a wheel rivet set punch on the rivets and deliver blows until the spokes are tight, continuing around the hub until all are tight.

Questions:

1. Why is it necessary to have the inside of the wheel up when placed on the wheel rack ready to receive the tire?
2. Why do we mark the tire?
3. Why is it unnecessary to count the revolutions of the tire measuring wheel as it goes around the rim?
4. Why should the tire be cooled before measuring when an accurate job is required?
5. Why is it necessary to open up bolt holes with a wood drill?
6. What is the appearance of the spokes at the hub when they are loose?
7 What are the indications of a rim bound condition of the wheel?
8. What are the purposes of the felloe plate?

RENEWING WAGON AND BUGGY TIRES

Directions:

1. Remove the old tire and prepare the wheel to receive the new one by renewing broken spokes and rims, and wedging spokes, as in the case of setting tires.

2. Curve the end of the new tire with a hammer and place it in the tire bender, Figs. 69 and 70, and bend to approximately the curvature of the wheel.

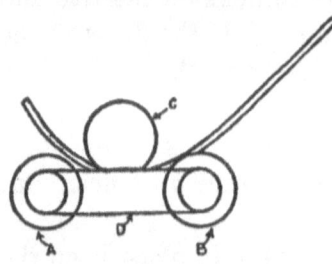

FIG. 69. A, roller driven by handle geared to it; D, chain which drives roller B; C, adjustable roller for giving different curvatures.

3. Drive a large block of wood between two spokes that have an opening in the rim between them until all the opening in the rim is at one joint.

4. Place the zero graduation mark of the tire-measuring wheel even with the right side of the opening.

5. Travel around the wheel to the right *counting* the revolutions of the wheel as you do so.

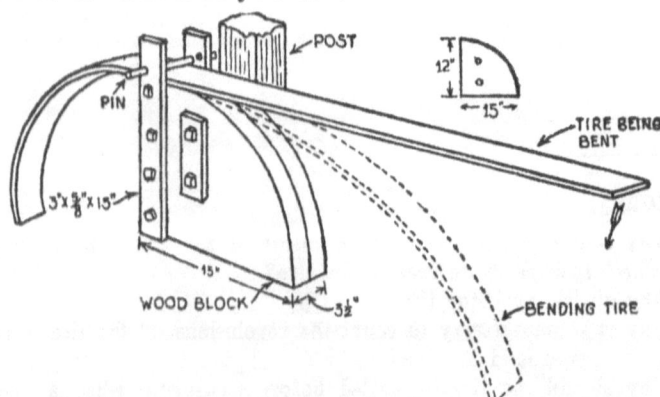

FIG. 70. A very satisfactory bender for a small shop.

6. Continue around the wheel when the tire-measuring wheel crosses the starting point or opening stop.

Operation No. 37
Page No. 2

7 Set the pointer of the measuring wheel even with the left side of the joint.

8. Place the bent tire down over your head with one side resting on the forge and the other on the anvil.

9. Set the zero graduation mark of the measuring wheel even with the right end of the tire as you face the opening. Fig. 71.

10. Travel to the right around the tire, counting the revolutions as you do so, until as many revolutions have been counted as were counted in measuring the wheel and, in addition, travel until the pointer rests on the tire. Mark the tire at this point.

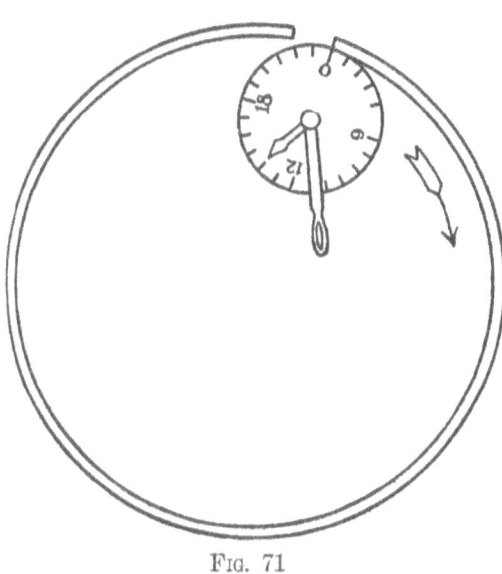

FIG. 71

11. Cut the tire off with a hot or cold cutter a distance to the right of this mark equal to the thickness of the tire to allow for welding.

12. Prepare the end of the tire for welding by making an abrupt bevel on the top side of both ends. Be

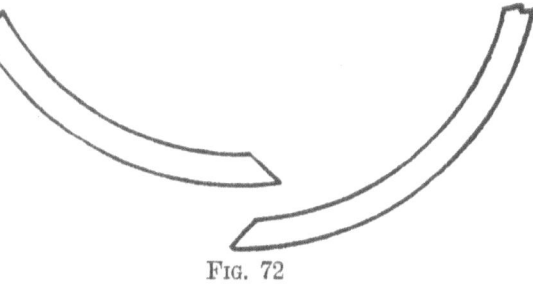

FIG. 72

careful not to allow the bevel to exceed one and one-half times the thickness of the stock. Turn the tire down on edge and hammer on the edge of the bevel until the point of the scarf is slightly narrower than the heel. Fig. 72.

13. Spring the tire until the beveled ends are exactly even but one is about four inches directly over the other

14. Flux the ends while red hot, and spring the tire until the end that is highest can be pushed under the one that is lowest. Lap the ends slightly more than the length of the bevel and hammer on the heel of the top bevel until the tire is in line and the ends fit together   Fig. 73.

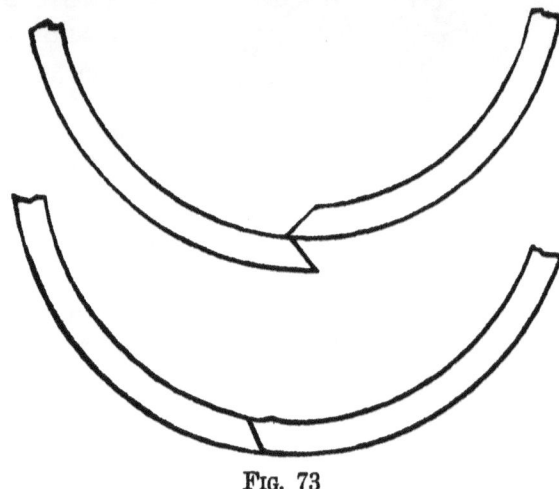

FIG. 73

15. Place it in the fire and take heat very slowly

16. Turn off the blast occasionally so that the top end will be heated as fast as the bottom end.

17 When both ends are to a welding heat remove to the anvil and deliver blows until the ends are stuck. Then turn on its side and hammer the edge until the tire is uniform in width.

18. Take another heat and dress down the weld.

19. Measure, then shrink or stretch the tire until it is the required size for the wheel.

20. Put the tire on the wheel as directed in Operations No. 35 and No. 36.

21. In cases where tires are to be bolted on, mark the tire with a center punch at points where the holes are required. Drill with the required size drill and countersink holes to fit the bolt heads.

Operation No. 38

RENEWING WAGON FELLOES

Directions:

1. Remove the tire and place the wheel on the bench wheel rack, the point of the hub up.

2. Screw the wheel down, saw thru the crack at the ends of the broken felloe and remove the broken felloe by hammering on the inside of the felloe alternately on each side of the spokes.

3. Choose a felloe that has the same curvature, the same width, the same thickness, and one that is slightly longer than the one removed.

4. Lay a new felloe flat on the spoke tenons, the inside edge resting against the shoulders of the spokes and the ends extending slightly past the ends of the two adjacent felloes. Mark the top of the felloe to indicate the top side.

5. Hold the felloe in this position and make pencil marks across on the underside of the new felloe at the points where it laps on the old. Make marks across the underside of the felloe on each side of the spoke tenons.

6. Use a try square to make a straight line across the ends of the felloes at the points marked, and square guide lines across the face.

7 Saw off the ends leaving all of the pencil lines on the felloe.

8. Clamp the felloe in the vise with the inside toward you, the jaws of the vise resting on the sides of the felloe, and the guide lines locating a hole for one of the tenons above the vise and in a convenient position for boring. Select a bit the size of a tenon, center it carefully from left to right on the inside of the felloe and with the point exactly in the center between the two tenon guide lines, bore the hole. Be careful that the bit keeps the direction of the guide lines and does not change the direction, right or left. Repeat these operations for the other holes.

9. Put the felloe on the tenons of the spokes and drive them down by hitting first over one hole and then the other.

10. When the ends of the felloe tend to wedge, run a saw thru between the ends.

11. Continue to run the saw thru and hammer over the holes until the felloe rests firmly on the shoulder of the spokes.

12. With a chisel split the ends of the spokes crosswise of the felloe and wedge with hickory wedges.

13. Put a clamp on the felloe at the joints to hold them in position and with a ⅜" bit bore a hole thru the end of the felloes, forming a 45 degree angle with the joint.

14. Insert a dowel pin, remove the clamp, saw off the dowel and dress down the new felloe with a wood rasp until it conforms to the shape of the old felloe.

Questions:

1. Why bore the tenon holes from the inside of the felloe?
2. Why use wood instead of iron dowels?
3. In inserting a new felloe why cut it slightly longer than the distance between the ends of the old felloe?
4. What is the purpose of dowels?
5. Why split the tenons crosswise of the felloes in wedging?

RENEWING HALF RIMS

Directions:

1. Remove the tire from the wheel and screw the wheel down on the bench wheel rack, the point of the hub up.

2. Remove the old half rim by striking blows on the inside of the rim on either side of the spokes. Strike the inside of the rim near each spoke so that the rim slips off all of the spoke tenons at the same time.

3. Renew any spokes that may be broken or worn badly at the tenons.

4. If the shoulders of the spokes at the tenon are slightly worn, square all shoulders very slightly with a tenoner or hollow auger

5. Choose a half rim that is the same width, thickness, and curvature as the old one and one whose ends extend slightly past the ends of the other half when it is held in place on the tenons.

6. Clamp the new half rim in position so that its ends extend over the ends of the half rim remaining on the wheel and the rest of it lies on top of the tenons and against the shoulders of the tenons. Mark the rim so as to indicate the top side. With a pencil in the right hand and your left side to the wheel, back around the new half rim meanwhile pressing the rim firmly down against the shoulder on the tenon and marking on the under side lines across the rim on either side of the tenon. Continue until the location for all the holes in the rim are marked and then mark the length by marking across the under side of the new rim even with the ends of the old.

7 Clamp the rim in the vise inside of the curve toward you and the jaws of the vise on the sides of the rim.

8. Choose a bit the same size of the tenon on the spokes. Place the bit in the center of the width of the rim and exactly

half the way between the two guide lines. Bore straight thru in the direction of the guide lines.

9. Slip the rim up in the vise and repeat these operations until all the holes are bored.

10. Square a line across the face of the rim at the end where the length was marked and saw off, leaving all the mark on the rim.

11. Start the rim on the tenons, beginning at one end. When one tenon is started, go to the next spoke. Bend it until the tenon will start in the hole. If the ones that have been started tend to pull out when the next ones are being started drive the rim on a little farther Continue until all the tenons are started in the holes, then strike alternately on all the holes until the ends of the new rim strike the ends of the old. When the ends begin to wedge, run a saw between them.

12. Continue to run the saw thru between the ends and drive down the rim until it rests firmly on the shoulders of the tenons and the ends slide loosely past each other

13. Split the ends of the tenons crosswise of the rim with a thin chisel and start hickory wedges. Strike the wedges, then rim until the rim rests firmly on the shoulders and all the tenons are tight. If during the wedging process the wheel tends to become rim bound continue to run the saw between the ends.

14. Dress down the new rim with a wood rasp until it conforms in shape to the old rim.

Questions:

1. Why bore the tenon holes from the inside of the half rim?

2. Why is it necessary to hold the rim firmly against the shoulder on the tenon when marking the location of the tenon holes?

3. Why is it necessary to start all the tenons in the tenon holes before any of them are driven up?

4. Why is it necessary to have the rim rest firmly on the shoulder before the wedge is tightened?

Operation No. 40

REPLACING SPOKES

Directions.

1. If a wagon spoke is to be replaced, remove the tire, clamp the wheel on the bench wheel rack, and remove the rim or felloe. Grasp the stub of the old spoke and with a heavy hammer strike a flat blow on top of the spoke near the hub. Continue to strike with a lighter blow meanwhile bending the spoke up and down as far as it will go. As soon as it is loose in the hub grasp with both hands, work up and down, and pull out.

2. If the tenon breaks off in the hub choose a wood drill slightly smaller than the thickness of the tenon and bore holes close together the entire width of the tenon, being careful to keep the bit pointed toward the center line of the hub. With a flat chisel about the width of the thickness of the broken tenon, clean out the mortise.

3. Choose a spoke the required length and size. Gage the depth of the mortise and cut the tenon slightly shorter than the depth and fit to the mortise.

4. If the wheel has a considerable dish, cut off a little of the under side of the tenon until the spoke will be in line with the other spokes when driven home.

5. Drive a spoke into the hub until the shoulder of the spoke rests on the hub.

6. Set a steel framing square with the corner against the hub band and the longest side extending along one of the old spokes. Mark on the blade the location of the shoulder and the end of the felloe tenon.

7. Transfer these locations to the new spoke and saw off the spoke to length.

8. Point the end of the spoke with a spoke pointer and cut the tenon with a hollow auger down to the mark locating the shoulder.

9. Hold the hollow auger level so that the shoulder of the

tenon will be formed exactly at right angles to the sides of the spoke.

10. If a buggy spoke is to be replaced, first cut off the head of the rivet in the hub that holds the old spoke in and drive it out with a small punch. Remove the old spoke by hammering on the top near the hub and working the end of old spoke up and down until it is free.

11. If the V part of the new spoke tenon is larger than the V on the old spoke, dress it to the size of the old spoke with a wood rasp.

12. Put in the spoke and lay it out, and cut the tenon in the same manner as in replacing the wagon spoke.

13. After the tire has been replaced bore or burn out the rivet holes and replace the hub rivets.

Questions:

1. How is the depth of the mortise in the hub gaged?
2. What is the result of trying to insert a spoke whose V-shaped tenon is larger than the V tenon on the spoke removed?
3. Why cut the hub tenon shorter than the depth of the mortise?
4. How are spokes made secure in the hub?
5. Why should a hollow auger be held in line with the spoke while cutting the tenon?
6. How are the sizes of a hollow auger marked?
7. How are hollow augers adjusted to size?
8. Why use a spoke pointer before cutting a tenon?
9. How may a new spoke be made to conform in the dish to an old spoke?
10. Why burn a hole before replacing wheel rivets?

PAINTING REPAIRED PARTS

Directions:

1. Be sure that the wood is thoroly dry.

2. Rub down the surface with No. 1 sandpaper until it is smooth and clean. Brush off all dust.

3. Apply a priming coat of linseed oil in which is mixed a little pigment such as red lead or ochre. Two or three pounds of pigment to the gallon is sufficient.

4. If the brush is dry at the beginning saturate it by dipping it into the paint for about two-thirds of its length and wiping out the paint on the edge of the bucket. After the brush is saturated dip it into the paint each time, about one-third the length of the bristles and before removing from the bucket slap it lightly against the sides to remove any excess of paint and to properly distribute the paint thru the bristles. As the brush is removed from the bucket, point the bristles slightly upward.

5. Hold the brush loosely in the hand with the handle vertical to the surface being painted. Do not permit the brush to drag more than one-third the length of the bristles. Make long even strokes in the direction of the grain of the wood with the broad side of the brush. Begin in the corners and lead with the edge of the brush instead of the broad side. When painting in corners place the brush against the surface, near the corner, leaning the handle away from the corner at an angle of about 45 degrees. Press on the brush until the bristles are bent over about one-third of their length and then push the ends of the bristles into the corner. While the brush is being pushed into the corner give it a slight shaking motion to spread the paint, and then give an outward brush stroke. Brush the paint out well and evenly over the entire surface.

6. Allow each coat to become thoroly dry before applying the next coat.

7 Just before applying the second coat, putty up nail holes and other imperfections. White lead mixed with whiting is best for this, but ordinary putty mixed with linseed oil will do.

8. When thru with the job clean the brush thoroly by washing it out in turpentine or benzine. If the brush is to be used again in the same color of paint it may be kept suspended in a can of water without cleaning out the paint, or it may be left in the paint covered with linseed oil.

Questions:

1. Why should the wood be thoroly dry before it is painted?
2. Why should all dust be removed from the surface?
3. What is the purpose of a priming coat?
4. What is the purpose of the pigment in the priming coat?
5. Would white lead made quite thin with oil give a satisfactory priming coat? Why?
6. What is the effect of dipping the brush too deeply into the paint?
7 Why point the bristles slightly upward when removing the brush from the bucket?
8. Why should each coat become thoroly dry before applying the next coat?
9. Why should putty never be applied before priming?
10. Why wash out the brush in turpentine or benzine?

Operation No. 42

SHARPENING PLOW SHARES

Directions:

1. Place the share in the fire, bar down, and the share standing straight up. Slip it thru the fire until the end of the bar and the point will be heated first.

2. When the end is up to a bright red heat remove it from the fire, place on an anvil bar lying flat and the share sticking straight up. In this position strike blows on the end of the point until it is square. When the point upsets place it flat on the anvil and draw it down. Fig. 74.

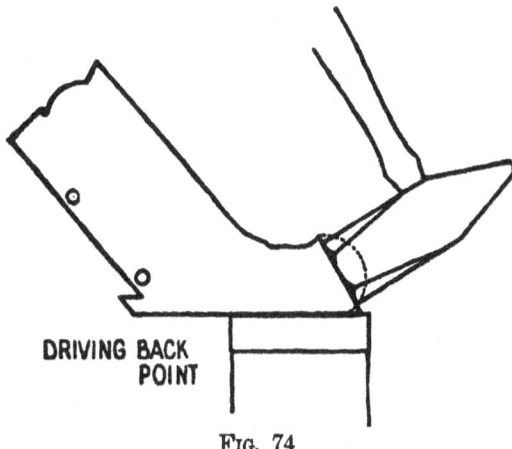

FIG. 74

3. If the plow point is slightly split heat and upset it a small amount at the point. Flux the point, replace in the fire and raise to a welding heat. Remove it from the fire, place it flat on the anvil and weld down smooth.

4. Continue to hammer alternately on the end and on the top until the point is square instead of rounded and a line across the point forms slightly less than a right angle with the bar side. Hammer or file the top of the point until it is tapered abruptly, to a 45 degree angle. The point should be turned toward the bar side about 1/8 inch to 1/4 inch as a "landing." Fig. 75.

5. Return it to the fire with the cutting edge down and the edge of the point over the tuyere. Heat to a bright red, remove from the fire and turn upside down on the anvil so that the side of the point rests flat on the anvil. With a peen or cross-peen hammer draw out the cutting side of the point to a thin edge for three or four inches. Fig. 76. Heat further

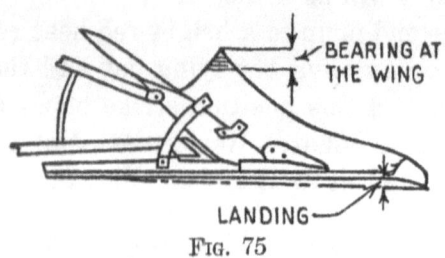

Fig. 75

back toward the heel of the share and repeat the operation. On the third and following heats, place the share flat on the anvil right side up and the cutting edge lengthwise of the

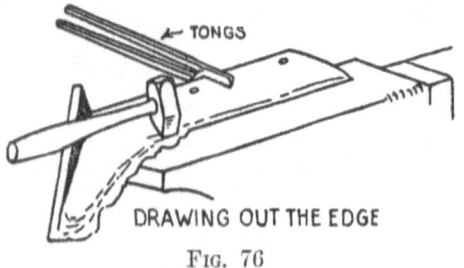

Fig. 76

anvil. In this position, draw it to a thin cutting edge. As the drawing proceeds toward the heel slip the cutting edge nearer the edge of the anvil while drawing. Continue until the entire cutting edge is drawn out. Give a plow suction by inclining the point downward about $1/4''$ to $3/8''$ Fig. 77   To prevent the cutting edge from flaring at the heel strike it on the end before the heel is drawn out. Place it on the surface plate or floor plate and level it. From $3/4''$ to $1 1/4''$ depending upon the size of the plow of the outer corner of the share should rest on the surface plate for "bearing." The share

Operation No. 42
Page No. 3

will then rest on three points, the heel of the bar, the point and the outer wing of the share. Fig. 78.

To harden the share draw the cutting edge slowly thru the fire until it is to a very low red heat about $\frac{1}{4}''$ from the cut edge, then plunge, point first, into water

If too much heat is in the plow share it will crack or break.

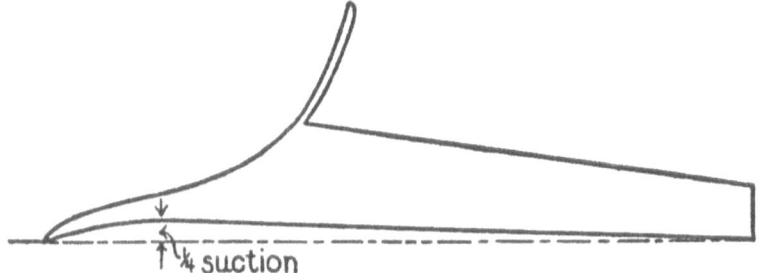

Fig. 77

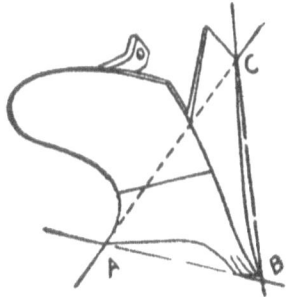

Fig. 78

References.:

Jones, *Forging and Smithing*, p. 166.

Questions:

1. Why should a plow share be placed on a face plate frequently during the process of sharpening?

2. Why should the edge of the share be near the edge of the anvil while it is being drawn out?

POINTING A PLOW

Directions:

1. Examine the worn point to determine how much of a point will be needed to bring the share to its original length, and to the width required. Fig. 79.

2. Heat the point of the share to a bright red heat, place it on the anvil, bar down, and the share sticking up, and deliver upsetting blows on the point. When the point is upset to about ¼" in thickness, lay it flat on the anvil and hammer to a feather edge.

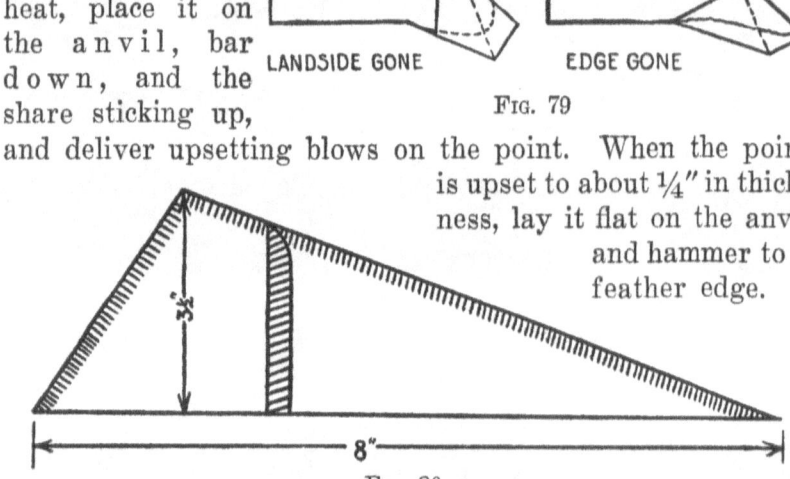

Fig. 79

Fig. 80

3. Use an old rasp or a piece of old plowshare for repointing. Heat the piece to a bright red heat, place on the edge of the anvil and forge to approximately the shape and dimensions shown in Fig. 80. Draw the short sides of the point to a feather edge but leave the long side about ¼" thick, as shown by the cross-section on the figure.

4. Build a large, clean fire and have a good supply of coke on the forge so that the fire may be replenished as often as necessary

5. Place the point of the share in the fire, bar down, and raise it slowly to a bright red heat. Remove it from the fire and flux the bottom of the bar about three or four inches back

from the point and replace it in the fire. Grasp the wide end of the point in the tongs and extend the narrow end into the fire, being careful to place the point about parallel with the bottom of the fire so that the end of the point will not be burned off. As soon as the point is to a bright red heat for a distance of four inches from the end, remove it from the fire and place it flat on the anvil, the thick edge to the right. Flux it for about four inches from the end.

6. Replace it in the fire alongside the share and raise both to a welding heat. If the point heats faster than the share remove the point until the share catches up.

7 As soon as both have a white molten appearance have the helper remove the share from the fire, strike it on the anvil, and very quickly place it on the anvil, the bottom of the bar up and the point of the share extending to within about an inch of the side of the anvil nearest you. As the helper is doing this, remove the point from the fire, strike it on the anvil and rest it on the edge of the anvil, the thick edge toward the bar side of the share, so that it forms a 45 degree angle with the face of the anvil and extends above the edge about five inches and is directly over the bar. Lower it on the bar, being careful that the thick edge of the point falls exactly even with the outside edge of the bar and the point extends about four inches onto the bar. Fig. 81.

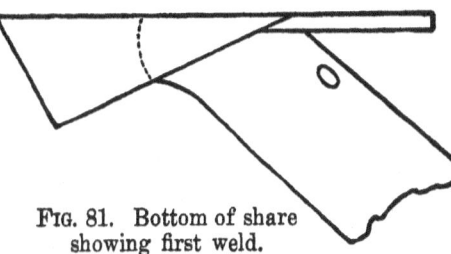

FIG. 81. Bottom of share showing first weld.

8. Deliver first light then heavy blows until the point is firmly welded to the bar

9. Place the share on the bottom and slip it thru the fire until the point of the share is over the tuyere. Raise it very slowly to a welding heat from the bottom side. Remove it from the fire, place it flat on the anvil, the top of the share up, and deliver blows on the point of the share until it is welded firmly to a new point.

10. While the point is still a bright red turn it upside down on the face of the anvil and have the helper hold the sledge on the end of the share directly over the anvil, and with a hammer bend the end of the point over the edge of the anvil. Make this bend a distance from the point of the share that will give the point the desired additional length. After making a right angle bend, flux the top of the share and bend the point down flat on the share. Hammer on the top of the new point until it lies flat on the share and its edge coincides exactly with the edge of the bar   Fig. 82.

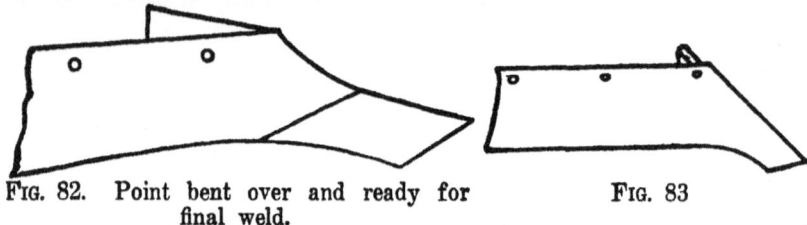

FIG. 82. Point bent over and ready for final weld.   FIG. 83

11. Place the share in the fire, bar down, and raise it slowly to a bright red heat. Remove it and sprinkle flux in the cracks between the points and the share. Replace in the fire, bar down, and raise it very slowly to a welding heat. Remove it from the fire, place it flat on the anvil, the top of the share up, and with heavy blows weld the point down along the thick edge. Sprinkle a small amount of flux between the thin edge and the share and hammer the thin edge down until it rests flat on the share.

12. Continue to take heats and hammer the weld until the point is firmly welded to the share.

13. After the point is firmly welded on the top, turn the share over and with a peen or cross-peen hammer weld any projecting or unwelded edges down to the throat of the share.

14. Trim the point with a hot cutter until it conforms in shape to Fig. 83, and sharpen.

References:

Jones, *Forging and Smithing*, p. 166.

EXAMINATION OF HORSES' FEET PREPARATORY TO SHOEING

Directions:

1. Stand in front of the horse and look straight at the front of his hoofs to see if the hoofs are straight, toeing in or toeing out. Fig. 84.

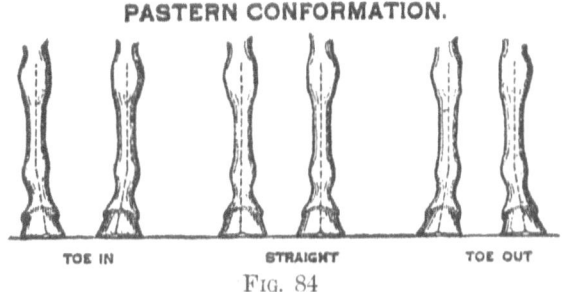

FIG. 84

2. Step to one side and examine the foot to see if it is regular, sloping, or stumpy   Fig. 85.

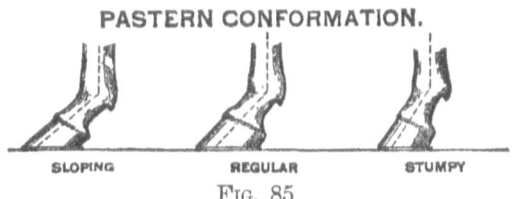

FIG. 85

3. Make an examination for broken or split hoofs or for any other defects that may be seen without raising the hoof.

4. Since defects in travel can be corrected somewhat by shoeing, watch the horse as he travels to see whether he throws his feet in or out or whether he over-reaches with his hind feet.

5. Raise each foot and examine the bottom and the frog for defects.

6. To raise the foot, walk gently up to the horse about even with his shoulders.

7. Turn your back to the horse's head and place the hand next to him on his shoulder.

8. In this position run the hand down the back of his leg until his fetlock is reached. With thumb and fingers pinch the tendons in the leg above the fetlock. Usually the horse will raise his foot with this inducement.

9. If he refuses to raise his foot, press gently with your body against his shoulder and lift the foot.

10. Stand close to the horse, straddle the foot and hold it between your legs just above your knees.

11. If the hind foot is to be raised, stand with the back to the horse's head, even with the flank.

12. Place the inside of the hand on the horse's hip and press gently; meanwhile run the other hand down the back of the horse's leg past the hock and grasp the tendons above the hoof.

13. Press harder against the hip until the horse's weight is on the opposite leg, then raise the foot, and as you do so walk forward a step and swing your inside leg under the horse's leg until the hoof rests even with your knees.

References:

Manual for Army Horseshoers, p. 48.

Questions:

1. What are the indications that a horse interferes?
2. What are the indications that he over-reaches or forges?
3. Why walk gently up to a horse?
4. Why should a strange horse be handled cautiously but firmly?
5. Why press against the horse's shoulder while raising his foot?
6. Why be careful as to the position in which the horse's foot is held when it is raised?

REMOVING OLD SHOES

Directions.

1. Raise the foot, and with the clinch cutter and hammer straighten out the clinches by driving the thin edge of the clinch cutter under the clinches.

2. Hold the foot firmly and force the jaws of the pull-off pinchers under the shoe between the heel and the first nail hole.

3. Close the handles of the pinchers until the jaws meet under the shoe and push the handles toward the toe of the shoe and slightly toward the center of the hoof.

4. As soon as one side has been pried away from the hoof a short distance put the pinchers on the other side of the shoe near the heel, and repeat.

5. Continue working toward the toe until the shoe is entirely free from the hoof.

References:

Manual for Army Horseshoers, p. 51.

Questions:

1. Why should the clinches be cut before removing the shoe?
2. Why begin at the heel in removing a shoe?

PREPARING HOOF FOR SHOE

Directions

1. Support the foot by placing the palm of the left hand under the hoof. Use the shoeing knife in the right hand to clean all of the chalky substance from the bottom of the foot out to the wall or the horn. Do not cut the frog except to trim slightly the frayed parts.

2. Remove the rim or wall around the outside of the foot with the hoof nippers as follows: Grasp the handles of the nippers and place them on the hoof so that the blunt jaw is on the outside and the cutting jaw is on the inside of the rim of the hoof, and the handles are perpendicular to the bottom of the hoof. With the nippers in this position cut thru the wall to a depth that will leave the rim of the hoof slightly higher than the sole of the foot.

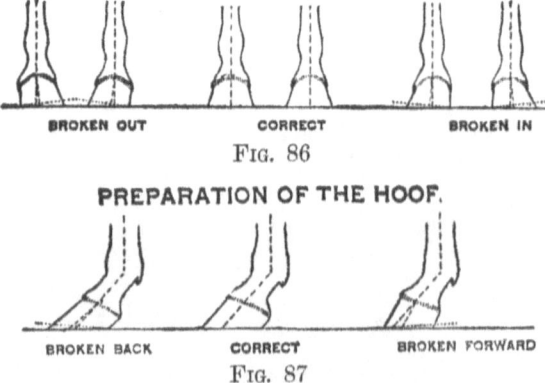

PREPARATION OF THE HOOF.

BROKEN OUT   CORRECT   BROKEN IN

FIG. 86

PREPARATION OF THE HOOF.

BROKEN BACK   CORRECT   BROKEN FORWARD

FIG. 87

3. Exercise great care and continue cutting until all the rim is approximately level and is a little higher than the sole of the foot from the heel to the toe.

4. Use the rough side of the rasp to level the foot. Level the right side of the foot by directing the rasp toward the toe. Level the left side by directing the rasp toward the heel.

Operation No. 46
Page No. 2

5. When the foot is approximately level, place the fitted and leveled shoe on the hoof in position. If there is a crack between the shoe and the hoof take off the high places until the shoe rests on the wall all the way around.

6. If the shoe rocks on the foot locate the high places and proceed cautiously to rasp them down.

7 Be very careful in cutting away the horn at the heel to prevent the wall at the heel from being lowered below the sole of the foot.

8. If the foot toes out, cut as much as possible from the wall on the outside of the foot, leaving the inside high. If the foot toes in, cut more of the inside, leaving the outside high. Fig. 86.

9. If the foot is stumpy, cut as much as possible from the heel without cutting below the sole. If the foot is too sloping cut a maximum amount off the toe. Fig. 87.

References:
Manual for Army Horseshoers, p. 51.

FITTING HORSE SHOES

Directions.

1. If a shoe is to be toe calked, heat it to a bright red heat on the toe and strike it on the sides until the heels are about an inch apart. Place the shoe flat on the anvil, grooved side up, with the sides parallel to the edge of the anvil and the toe to the left. Grasp the required kind of toe calk in the tongs and place it across the toe of the shoe far enough back from the toe so that all the toe calk is on the shoe and none extends over the edge of the shoe. Hold the toe calk in this position and strike a heavy blow directly over the spur on the toe calk. Strike another blow over the spur Do not strike the toe calk more than two heavy blows.

2. Place the toe of the shoe in the fire with the grooved side to the left and the heel inclined about 45 degrees to the right.

3. When heated to a yellow heat remove it and flux with borax and flux, and return to the fire.

4. Just before removing it from the fire to weld, turn the shoe over so that the toe calk is on the under side.

5. Leave it in this position a few seconds, remove from the fire, place it flat on the anvil or in the toe swage and weld down.

6. While the toe of the shoe is still hot, open up the nail holes in the shoe to the required size with pritchel punching from the hoof side of the shoe.

7 Then open up the nail hole on the groove side of the shoe so that the nails can be driven into the groove.

8. In opening up the nail holes with a pritchel incline the top of the pritchel toward the inside of the shoe about ten degrees.

9. Heat the heels of the shoe and bend them out so that they are parallel for about two inches from the tips.

10. Reheat and place on the face of the anvil, the groove

Operation No. 47
Page No. 2

of the shoe down, so that about 1½" of the ends stick over the edge.

11. Bend the projecting ends until they form a right angle with the rest of the shoe.

12. Turn the shoe over on the face of the anvil and strike a heavy blow on the top of the calks. Direct this blow so that the calk will be bent slightly toward the toe calk and also toward the outside of the shoe.

13. Hammer on the top and on the sides of the calks until they are the desired height and shape.

14. Level the shoe by placing it across the face of the anvil, calks down, and striking around the shoe where it is to come in contact with the foot.

15. With the shoe on the anvil, groove side up, and the heels toward you, place the pritchel in the nail hole on the right side and carry the shoe to the horse's foot. Lay the shoe on the bottom of the foot and examine it to see where it needs reshaping to make it conform in shape to the white line around the foot just inside of the rim.

16. Make the shoe as wide in the heel as the gait of the horse will permit without interfering.

17 Shape the shoes so that when the nails are driven in they will penetrate the horn instead of the sole of the foot.

References:

Manual for Army Horseshoers, p. 57

Questions:

1. Why bend the heels of the shoe together before welding on the toe?
2. Why should the toe calk not be struck after the spur is driven up?
3. Why place the shoe in the fire with the groove side to the left?
4. Why should the pritchel be inclined inward when opening the holes?
5. Why should the heels of the shoe be bent out until they are parallel before turning the calk?
6. Why should the finished heel calk be inclined slightly toward the outside of shoe?
7 Why should a shoe always be straightened by striking on the part that is to come in contact with the foot?
8. Why is the ground surface of the shoe plain and the upper surface concave?

NAILING ON SHOE

Directions:

1. Place the fitted, level shoe on the trimmed foot so that the center line of the shoe is in line with the center line of the form of the foot.
2. Push the shoe forward until the tip of the toe is in line with the front of the hoof.
3. Grasp a nail between the thumb and forefinger with the straight side of the nail toward the outside of the shoe.
4. With the other fingers and the palm of the left hand hold the shoe in position and place the nail straight side out in the second hole from the heel on the right hand side of the shoe.
5. Set the nail so that it is pointing toward a point on the top of the hoof about 1½" from the shoe.
6. Start driving the nail cautiously meanwhile letting the fingers extend over until they rest loosely on the place where the nail will come out. As soon as the tip of the nail comes out drive the nail up as far as it will go.
7. Bend the end of the nail down and twist it off by grasping it between the claws of the hammer and giving it a quick wrench.
8. Straighten the shoe on the foot and drive a nail in the other side.
9. Drive in other nails, twisting each one as soon as it is driven home, leaving only enough of the nail extending above the hoof to form a clinch.
10. When all the nails are driven, tighten the shoe by holding the clinch block under the cut end of each of the nails and delivering a couple of heavy blows on the heads.
11. Hold the foot in the clinching position, i.e. with the horse's leg stretched out in front, with the hoof resting on your knee, and cut off the ends of the nails with the nail nippers as close to the hoof as they can be conveniently cut.

Operation No. 48
Page No. 2

12. Run the corner of the rasp around the hoof just beneath the end of the nails, being careful not to file the nail.

13. Turn the clinches with a clinching tool or by holding the clinching block under the head and striking the cut end of the nail with the edge of the hammer face.

14. When all the clinches are turned, hammer them down flat.

15. Dress down the hoof with a rasp, being very careful not to file off the clinches.

16. When the projecting edges have been filed off even with the shoe run the corner of the rasp around the foot at the top of the shoe.

References:
Manual for Army Horseshoers, p. 64.

Questions:
1. Why should the shoe be pushed forward until the toe is in line with the top of the hoof?
2. When placing nails for driving, why should the straight side be out?
3. Why is the point of the nail bent slightly? Toward which side is it bent?
4. Why should a nail be driven cautiously until it comes thru on the top side of the hoof?
5. How does the bend of the point affect the direction the nail will take?
6. Why twist the ends of the nails off as soon as they are driven?
7. Why run the corner of the rasp beneath the ends of the nails before the clinches are turned?

INFORMATION TOPICS

LOCATION OF SHOP EQUIPMENT

All of the equipment in a blacksmith shop should be arranged so that the work to be done can be completed with the greatest ease and saving of time. The forge should be placed so that it is accessible from all sides and in a position

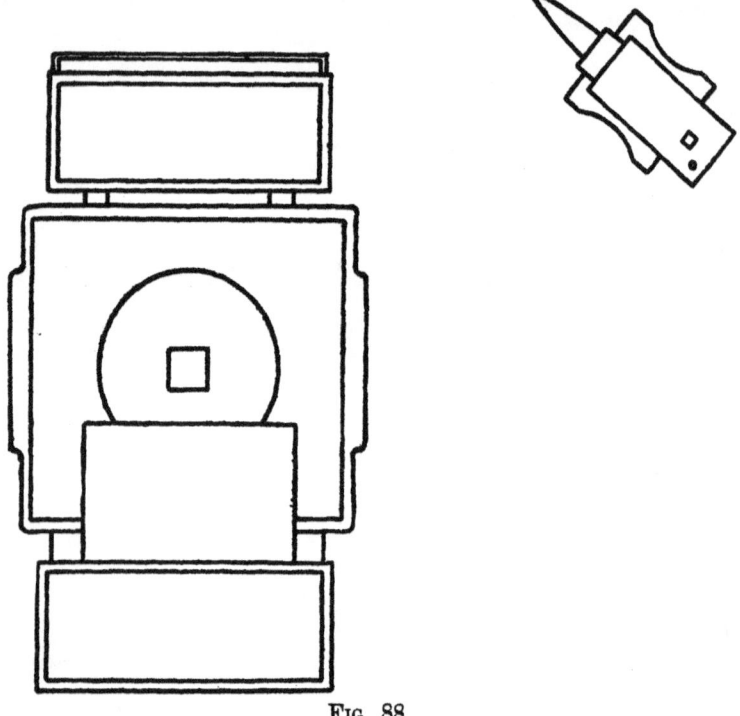

FIG. 88

where light is abundant. The tool rack may be a separate piece of equipment or it may be built on the side of the forge. The best position for the anvil is about three feet in front of the forge, and it should be placed so that the horn is to the left and the length of the anvil is at a 45 degree angle to the front of the forge. Fig. 88. When placed in this position the smith turns thru only 45 degrees in taking the hot iron from the forge to the anvil. The slack tub is located at the

Information No. 1
Page No. 2

left of the worker as he faces the forge. The vise bench should be located as near the forge as possible and should be built under a window if possible so that there will be an abundance of light. Such equipment as the tire-shrinker and drill should be placed with the idea of convenience and accessibility in mind.

If the shop is to be a combination iron and woodworking shop the iron working equipment should be located at one end, and the woodworking equipment, which should always include a bench fitted with a woodworking vise, located at the other end.

THE FORGE

In general, there are three types of forges used for heating iron and steel. Portable forges used in small repair shops and on construction jobs, forges built up of brick or concrete used by blacksmiths in smaller shops, cast-iron or sheet steel forges used in schools and in large commercial shops.

The parts common to all forges are the fire-pot and tuyere, the body and the hood. Fig. 89.

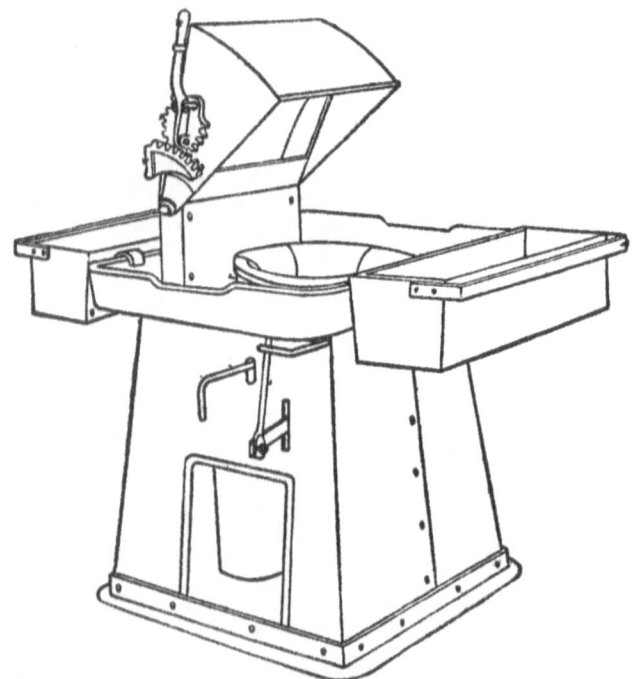

FIG. 89. A common type of school forge, using power blast and exhaust.

The fire-pot is a depression in the top of the forge hearth and serves to keep the fire from spreading.

The tuyere is at the bottom of the fire-pot at the terminus of the blast pipe and forms a sort of nozzle for distributing

Information No. 2
Page No. 2

the blast. The small openings at the top of the tuyere permit the passage of air and at the same time prevent ashes and cinders from dropping into the blast pipe. At the bottom of the tuyere is a door for cleaning out ashes or cinders. The adjustments of the tuyere are controlled by small rods extending from the tuyere to the front of the forge.

The hood of the forge is placed in such a position that it will collect the smoke from the fire.

Air is supplied to the fire in the ordinary blacksmith's type of forge, by means of a bellows or blower operated by hand, and attached to the side of the forge. The amount of blast is regulated by the speed of the bellows or fan. In school shops and large commercial shops the blast is usually supplied by a large fan which forces the air thru a system of pipes to the forges. The blast that enters the fire is regulated by a gate in the blast pipe just under the tuyere. This gate is operated by a handle conveniently placed in the front of the forge.

The forge with the hand blower probably is best for small work and it certainly is best for the beginner. The beginner almost invariably uses too much blast and burns his work and burns out his fire if he has power blast.

THE ANVIL

All blacksmith anvils are constructed alike, the only difference being the size and the materials from which they are made. The cheaper anvils are made entirely of cast-iron with chilled faces, but the best anvils are made of wrought-iron or of gun metal with tempered tool steel, wear resisting face. Anvils range in weight from 75 pounds to 400 pounds. The sizes most used range in weight from 150 to 250 pounds. Fig. 90.

The face of the anvil is slightly convex to facilitate the drawing of metal. The square hole in the face of the anvil near the heel is called the hardy-hole. It is used to hold the

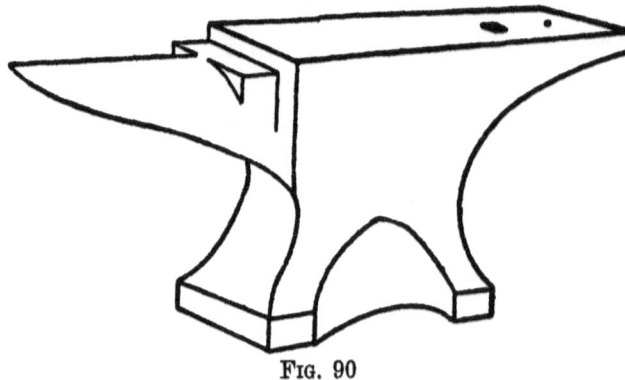

FIG. 90

hardy, the bottom fuller and the bottom swage. The round hole is called the pritchel hole and takes its name from the punch called the pritchel used by the smith for punching nail holes in horseshoes. The small, flat surface between the face of the anvil and the horn is called the chipping block and is used when it is desired to cut a piece of stock clear thru, and there is danger of the sharp edge of the tool coming in contact with the face of the anvil. The surface of the chipping block is soft and will not blunt the tool edge if it touches it. The horn is used in bending curves and in shaping rings and eyes.

The anvil should be fastened securely to an anvil block. This block may be of wood or cast-iron. The wood block is preferred by most smiths. If the wood block is used it should extend down into the ground about two feet. If the cast-iron block is used it should be fastened securely to the floor The block should be just high enough for the knuckles of the smith to come even with the top of the anvil as his arm hangs at his side.

The anvil is placed with the horn to the left, as you face it, for a right handed man. It should be so placed that the smith will face it by making one-third of a turn to the right from his position at the forge and it should be close enough for him to reach it without taking a step.

References:
  Bacon, *Forge Practice*, p. 6.

THE FORGE FIRE

There are two kinds of forge fires, namely, oxidizing and reducing.

An oxidizing fire is one to which more air is being supplied than is needed for the combustion of the fuel. In such a fire the excess of oxygen comes directly in contact with the iron or steel being heated, causing very rapid oxidation of the metal and, also tending to cool rather than heat. While the fire is in this condition welding is impossible, and any sort of heating is done with difficulty

The characteristics of an oxidizing fire are a very hollow appearance with a rim of live coals around the firepot, and a very thin layer of coals and cinders over the tuyere. Never permit your fire to become an oxidizing one.

A reducing fire is one that consumes all of the oxygen supplied by the blast. Such a fire is characterized by having a heavy compact bed of live coals over the tuyere banked well on three sides with wet, green coal. In a fire of this sort all of the oxygen supplied by the blast is utilized to make the fire hotter, and there is none to cause excess oxidation or to cool the iron or steel being heated.

Since a reducing fire is one of the most fundamental requirements for good forging the fire must be watched carefully As soon as it tends to become hollow or oxidizing it should be built up immediately

---

References:

Bacon, *Forge Practice*, p. 2.

FUEL USED FOR FORGE FIRE

For most work a good quality of smithing coal is used. For very large fires coke is used. Charcoal or coke fires are sometimes used in working tool steel and in cases where an unusually clean, even heat is required.

Good smithing coal is rather soft and should crumble easily in the hand. It should not split into layers and should be bright and glossy and show no dull streaks.

It should coke readily and be relatively free from sulphur and other impurities. Good coal will form very little clinker. It is quite impossible to do good work with poor coal.

Smithing coal may be purchased thru coal dealers or hardware houses. It usually is sold in 100-pound or 200-pound bags, but may be purchased by the ton if desired.

Neither domestic coal nor steaming coal is satisfactory for the forge.

References:
Ilgen, *Forge Work,* p. 4.

BLACKSMITH TOOLS

Tongs.

Tongs are classified according to the shape of the jaw as flat-jawed, bolt, and pick-up tongs. There are also many kinds of tongs with specially constructed jaws used for special

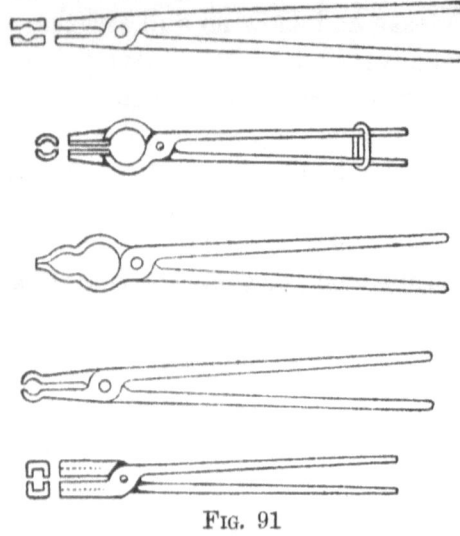

Fig. 91

purposes. The flat-jawed tongs are used primarily for handling flat or square stock, but they are provided with a groove down the inside of the jaw to permit the handling of round stock also. Bolt tongs are used for handling round stock only. Pick-up tongs, as the name implies, are used for picking up work and not for holding it while forging. Fig. 91.

Hammers.

Hand hammers are classified according to the shape of the peen as cross-peen, straight-peen, and ball-peen or machinists hammer They range in weight from 1½ to 4½ pounds. The class of work being done will determine the kind of hammer used. For all general purposes the cross-peen or straight-peen hammer is used, but for special kinds of work, such as forming depressions in sheet metal and truing up the inside of chain links after welding, the ball-peen hammer must be used. Fig. 92.

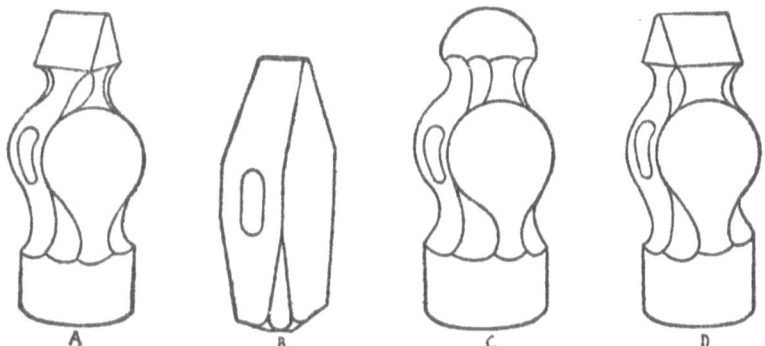

Fig. 92. Hammers, A and B, cross-peen; C, ball-peen; D, straight-peen.

Flatter.

The flatter is a tool made in the shape of a hammer with a handle and with a face about three inches square. It is used in connection with a helper with a sledge to smooth up the surfaces that cannot be conveniently smoothed with a hand hammer   Fig. 93.

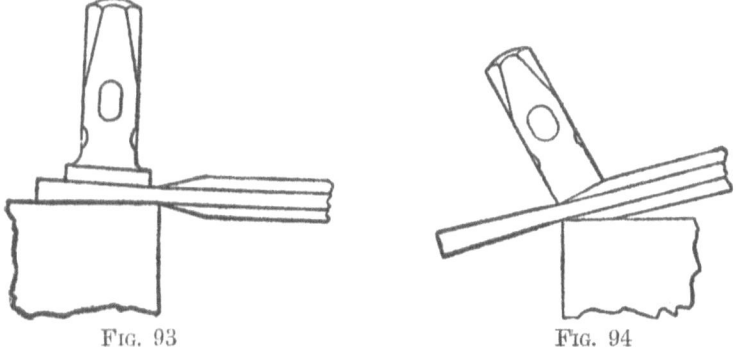

Fig. 93.   Fig. 94

Set Hammer

The set hammer is a square-faced hammer used by the smith where it is impossible to hit directly with a hand hammer. The set hammer is placed where it is desired to strike a blow and the top of it is struck with a sledge by a helper. One corner of the face of a set hammer is usually rounded so that a slightly rounded corner may be formed. Fig. 94.

Swages.

Swages are made up of two parts, a block having a semi-circular groove across its face and a square shank on the other side which fits in the hardy-hole. The other part is a hammer-shaped tool with a similar groove in its face and a top for striking with a sledge. They come in sizes from ¼" to 1½" and are used for rounding iron to its original size that has become distorted during the process of forging. Fig. 95.

Swage Block.

The swage block is made of cast-iron and weighs about 150 pounds. It is about 1½ feet square and about six or eight inches thick. The edges of the swage block are provided with many semi-circular grooves so shaped and designed to take the place of the bottom swage. There are many varied shaped holes in the body of the swage block to be used for forming depressions in sheet-metal, bending iron, etc. Fig. 96.

Fullers.

There are two kinds of fullers, top and bottom. The bottom fuller is a blunt wedge-shaped block of iron that fits into the hardy-hole. The top fuller is a hammer-shaped tool with a similar blunt wedge-shaped face and a top for striking with a sledge. They come in sizes ranging from ¼" to 1" and are used in connection with a sledge for forming grooves or making depressions in stock. Fig. 97

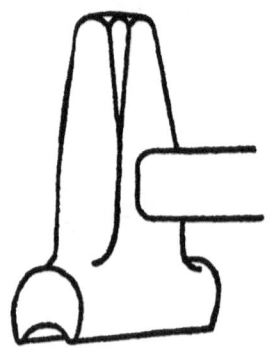

FIG. 95

Information No. 6
Page No. 4

Hot Cutter

The hot cutter is a thin, narrow, hatchet-shaped tool provided with a sharply beveled cutting edge and a top for striking with a sledge. When made it is usually tempered to refine the grain of the steel from which it is made. As its name implies, it is used for cutting hot metal. Fig. 98.

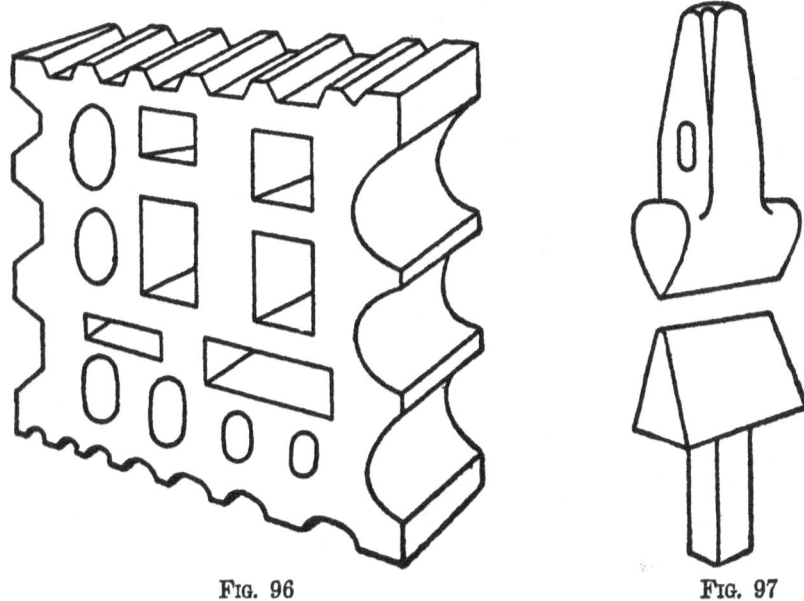

Fig. 96   Fig. 97

Cold Cutter.

The cold cutter is somewhat thicker than the hot cutter but of the same width of cutting edge. Its sides are somewhat bulged to give the additional strength necessary for cutting cold metal. It is always tempered and ground to a sixty-degree cutting edge, and is used in connection with a sledge for cutting cold stock. Fig. 99.

Hardy.

The hardy is a tool shaped somewhat like the cutters except that it has a square shank which fits into the hardy hole in the anvil. It is tempered, ground to a sixty degree cutting edge and is used to cut both hot and cold stock. Fig. 100.

Punches.

There are two kinds of punches, namely, handle and hand. The handle punch is used in connection with a sledge where large holes are to be punched in large stock. The hand punch is used for all small holes. The construction of the two kinds is similar to the part which functions to produce the hole, being ground so that the end is perfectly plane and the edge of the end sharp. They are made in special shapes for special purposes. Fig. 101.

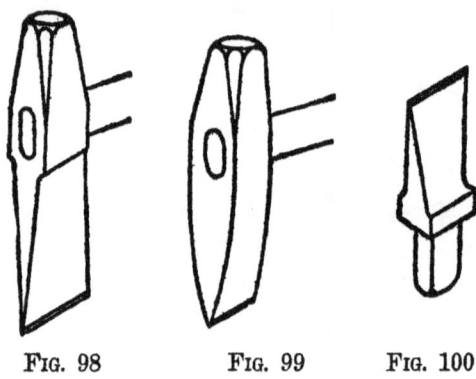

Fig. 98   Fig. 99   Fig. 100

Bench and Vise.

The blacksmith bench may be any of a great variety of sizes. The space in the shop will generally determine the size used. It is usually made large enough to carry a blacksmith's vise near one end, and a good sized drawer for small tools near the middle. The bench should be well made of heavy material. Fig. 102.

Sledges.

There are three standard types of sledges, namely, double-faced, straight-peen, and cross-peen. All of these types range in weight from eight to twelve pounds, and are provided with a handle from 30" to 36" long. Sledges are used to strike tools such as top swage, top fuller, and to aid the smith in doing heavy drawing. Fig. 103.

Information No. 6
Page No. 6

Cone Mandrel.

The cone mandrel is made of cast-iron and is from 2½ to 3½ feet high. It is about 2 inches in diameter at the top

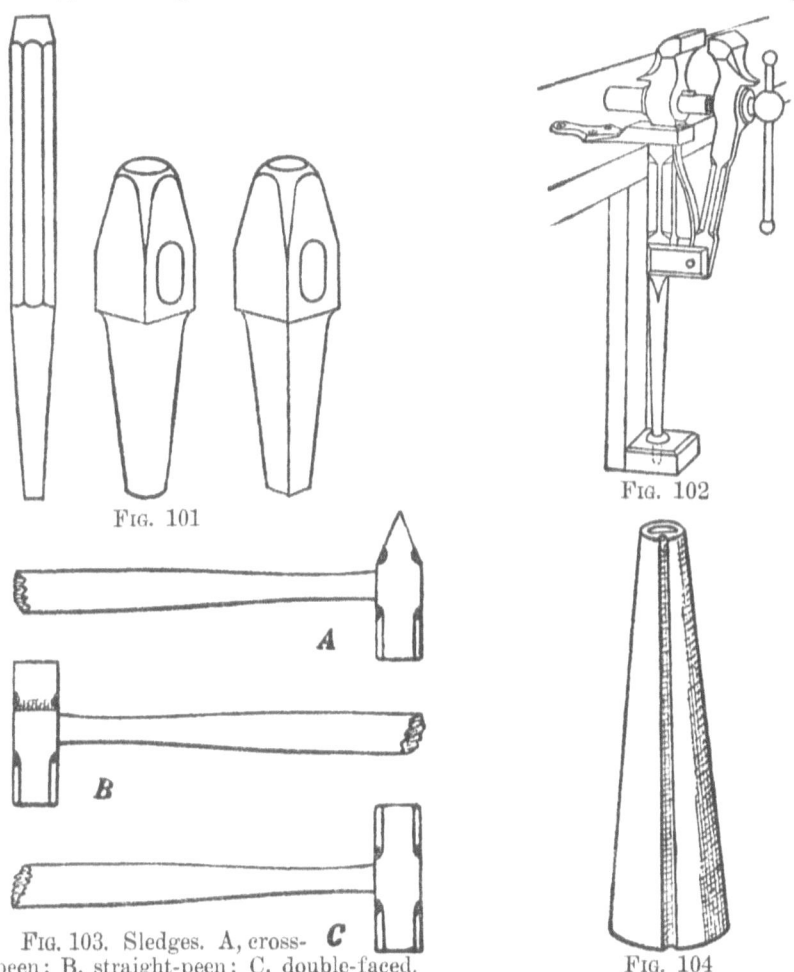

Fig. 101

Fig. 102

Fig. 103. Sledges. A, cross-peen; B, straight-peen; C, double-faced.

Fig. 104

and 14 inches at the bottom. It is used for truing rings. Fig. 104.

References:

Harcourt, *Elementary Forge Practice*, p. 21. Ilgen, *Forge Work*, p. 7

IRON AND STEEL

Cast-Iron.

Pig-iron is the product of the blast furnace and is the first step in the manufacture of cast-iron as well as all grades of iron and steel. Castings are made from pig-iron which has been remelted in a cupola and to which is sometimes added certain kinds of scrap iron to give the finished castings a desired quality Cast-iron contains from 2½% to 4½% carbon and a small percentage of impurities. It is granular in structure and brittle and cannot be forged. This form of iron cannot be welded in a forge fire.

Wrought-Iron.

Wrought-iron is pig-iron that has had all its carbon removed. It is fibrous in structure and can be bent to various shapes, cold as well as hot. It welds with ease without the use of flux. The purest form of wrought-iron is imported from Norway and Sweden and is known as Norway or Swedish iron. This grade of iron is used for classes of work that involves much bending or where a particularly high grade of material is required.

Soft Steel.

Soft steel is pig-iron that has had approximately all its carbon removed. The amount of carbon remaining in the iron will vary between the limits of .01 of 1% and .03 of 1%. This stock is used by the smith for making all sorts of forgings. It may be welded without the use of flux but it welds with greater ease when flux is used.

Tool Steel.

In the manufacture of tool steel all the carbon is first removed from pig iron and then a definite percentage of carbon is added. The precentage of carbon added determines the grade of steel and the various grades are referred to as being so many point carbon, the point being .01 of 1%. All tool steel will fall between the limits of 30 to 150 points.

Tool steel is of a chemical composition that will permit of its being hardened and tempered. Therefore it is used in the manufacture of tools. Tools that require toughness combined with hardness such as cold chisels, hammers, etc., are made from tool steel containing from 50 to 75 point carbon.

Tools such as lathe tools are made from tool steel containing from 75 to 100 point carbon. Taps, dies, reamer, etc., are made from 100 to 125 point carbon tool steel. Tools that require extreme hardness, such as razors, are made from tool steel whose carbon content ranges from 125 to 150.

References:

Harcourt, *Elementary Forge Practice*, p. 13. Bacon, *Forge Practice*, p. 159.

EFFECT OF HEAT ON STEEL

Tool steel contains a relatively high percentage of carbon and is therefore more susceptible to injury by heating than wrought-iron or mild steel. The higher the carbon content in tool steel, the lower the temperature at which it will burn. Tool steel should not be heated above a yellow heat except for welding.

The structure of tool steel is granular as compared with the fibrous structure of wrought-iron. As the carbon content increases in steel the more granular and brittle it becomes. This granular structure will change in its degree of coarseness as the temperature rises. It will reach its maximum degree of fineness at what is known as the critical temperature. The higher the percentage of carbon in tool steel, the lower the point at which the critical temperature is reached. After the critical temperature is reached further heating causes the granular structure to become coarse.

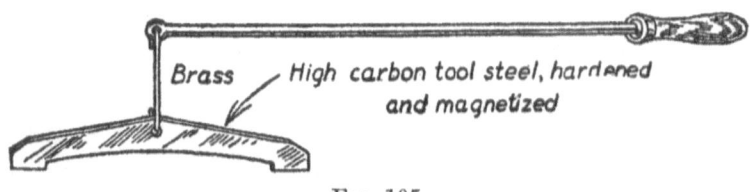

FIG. 105

There are two commonly used methods of determining the critical temperature of steel which are made use of by the blacksmith. The most commonly used method is to heat the piece of steel and make several nicks in it about an inch apart. Heat the steel thruout the nicked portion so that one end will be a yellow heat and the other to a cherry red. Plunge the piece quickly until cold. Break the bar at each nick and examine the fracture. The fracture that has the finest grain was at the critical temperature when cooled. The

Information No. 8
Page No. 2

color of the steel at this point is the color at which that particular grade of steel should be heated when hardening.

When tool steel reaches the critical temperature it is non-magnetic. This phenomenon forms the basis for the most accurate method of determining the critical temperature. While the temperature is being raised hold occasionally the end of a balanced bar magnet just over the part being heated. Just as soon as the end of the magnet is not attracted to the steel the critical temperature has been reached and the steel should be removed from the fire and plunged. Fig. 105.

References:
Harcourt, *Elementary Forge Practice*, p. 101.

WELDING

Welding is the most difficult of all the forging operations. It is accomplished by heating the metal until it is in a semi-molten or pasty condition, quickly placing the pieces in contact and hammering them until they are firmly united.

Wrought-iron and steel up to 50 point carbon can be welded readily, but the higher carbon steels and cast-iron can not be welded in the forge fire.

When a piece of iron or steel is heated even in a reducing fire more or less air will come in contact with it. The oxygen of the air will combine with the iron forming oxide of iron which will appear in the form of a scale on the metal. This oxide of iron has a higher melting point than the metal and if the structure of the metal will not permit of the temperature required to melt the scale, a flux must be used to prevent the formation of the scale, or, in the event of its having already formed, cause it to melt at a lower temperature. In general, steel will not permit of a temperature sufficiently high to melt the scale. It is therefore necessary to use a flux in welding materials of this sort.

The range of the welding temperature is very narrow The higher the percentage of carbon the shorter the range of welding temperatures. If the metal is heated to too high a temperature it will burn. Burning is indicated by a bright shower of exploding sparks coming from the fire. Burned iron is characterized by its rough pitted appearance. It is also crumbly and brittle.

The following are fundamental conditions for a good weld:

(1) The fire must be a perfectly clean reducing fire and should be built to accommodate the pieces being welded.

(2) The smith must know what he is going to do and exactly how he is going to do it before the heat is taken. Everything should be in readiness so that the weld can be

Information No. 9
Page No. 2

completed with the minimum loss of time after the heat is taken.

(3) The scarf must be so prepared that there is a good contact between the pieces, and thin edges should be avoided.

References:

Jones, *Forging and Smithing*, p. 133. Bacon, *Forge Practice*, p. 17

Questions:
 1. What is the difference between an oxidizing and a reducing fire?
 2. Why is it impossible to do welding in an oxidizing fire?
 3. Why can wrought-iron be welded without flux?
 4. What is the function of a flux?
 5. Why can not high carbon steels and cast-iron be welded in a forge fire?
 6. Why should everything be in readiness to complete the weld before the pieces are removed from the fire?
 7. Why should thin edges be avoided?

FLUXES

The principal functions of flux as used in welding are to prevent the formation of scale or oxide of iron on steel and to cause that which has already formed to melt at a lower heat. It is not in any sense a cement. Before two pieces of stock will unite, the oxide of iron must melt. In wrought-iron and soft steel the heat can be raised sufficiently to melt the scale without injury to the metal but in high quality soft steel and all tool steel the temperature required to melt the scale will injure the material. The higher the percentage of carbon in steel the more susceptible it is to injury by heat, so it is absolutely necessary in making any sort of weld in steel to use flux. Flux is also used as a covering for small or delicate work to prevent oxidation when the work must be reheated a number of times. Clean sand and borax are commonly used for flux. When mixed in the proportion of half and half they make a flux that will suffice for all ordinary welding. Prepared fluxes are much more expensive than a borax-sand flux but they are used by practically all blacksmiths. The quantity of flux required for a weld is so small that the cost is negligible.

References:
Harcourt, *Elementary Forge Practice*, p. 47

Questions:
1. Why should sand used for flux be very clean?
2. How does flux prevent oxidation of iron and steel?
3. What is the purpose of iron filings in prepared fluxes?
4. Why does stock with a high percentage of carbon burn at a lower temperature than material with a low percentage?

TEMPERING TOOL STEEL

When a piece of tool steel is heated to its critical temperature and is suddenly plunged into a cooling bath it becomes exceedingly hard and brittle. A tool having this extreme brittleness is not fit for use, but if it is heated up slowly the hardness will be drawn. The hardness may be reduced until it will conform to any requirement of the tool.

This process of reducing the hardness or brittleness of tools is called tempering. The particular degree of hardness at any time during the tempering process is indicated on the surface of the tool by what is known as temper colors.

When the tool is heated to the critical temperature, plunged and polished, it will assume a pearly gray color When this gray hardened surface is slowly heated, its color will change to a light straw If the heating is continued, its color will change as follows: light straw, dark straw, brownish purple, purplish blue, and blue. Each of these colors represents a different degree of hardness of the steel. Knowing the requirements of the tool, the smith is able to reduce the hardness to any point by watching the colors, then plunging the tool to fix the degree of hardness.

References:

Harcourt, *Elementary Forge Practice*, p. 101.

SHAPES AND SIZES OF WROUGHT-IRON, MILD STEEL, AND TOOL STEEL USED BY BLACKSMITHS

The shapes into which wrought-iron and mild steel are rolled for forge purposes are divided into three groups, namely, bar, strap, and sheet iron.

Bar iron is round, square, rectangular, half round, oval, or half oval in cross-section. Round, square, and rectangular are the shapes most frequently used by the smith and these shapes can be bought in a great variety of sizes and lengths.

The standard or usual sizes are as follows:

Round, diameter in inches, 3/16", 1/4", 5/16", 3/8", 7/16", 1/2", 9/16", 5/8", 3/4", 7/8", 1", 1 1/8", 1 1/4", 1 3/8", 1 1/2", 1 3/4", 2" and in 12 and 16-foot lengths.

Square, 3/8", 1/2", 9/16", 5/8", 3/4", 7/8", 1", 1 1/8", 1 1/4", 1 1/2", and in 12 and 16-foot lengths.

Rectangular or flat iron, in thicknesses ranging from 3/16" to 3/8" by sixteenths, and from 3/8" to 1" by eighths.

Flat iron that is 3/16" in thickness ranges in width from 1/2" to 1 1/4" by eighths, from 1 1/4" to 3" by quarters, and 3" to 6" by halves. In 1/4" thickness it ranges in width from 3/8" to 1 1/4" by eighths, from 1 1/4" to 3 1/2" by quarters and from 3 1/2" to 6" by halves. In 5/16" thickness it ranges in width from 5/8" to 1 1/2" by eighths, from 1 1/2" to 3" by quarters, from 3" to 6" by halves; 3/8" from 1/2" to 1 1/2" by eighths, from 1 1/2" to 2 1/2" by quarters and from 2 1/2" to 6" by halves; 1/2" iron from 3/4" to 1 1/2" by eighths, from 1 1/2" to 3" by quarters and from 3" to 6" by halves; 5/8" iron from 1" to 3" by quarters and from 3" to 6" by halves; 3/4" iron from 1" to 3" by quarters, 3" to 5" by halves, and from 5" to 6" by inches. One-inch iron comes in the following widths:

1 1/2", 2", 2 1/4", 3", 3 1/2", 4", 4 1/2", 5", and 6"

All of the above rectangular iron comes in 12 and 15-foot lengths.

Information No. 12
Page No. 2

The thickness of sheet iron is indicated by gage. The following is a list of standard gages with their equivalent in inches.

Gage	Inches	Gage	Inches
8	11/64	18	1/20
10	9/64	20	3/80
12	7/64	22	1/32
14	5/64	24	1/40
16	1/16		

Tool steel is rolled into round, square, rectangular or octagon bars. Round, square and octagon bars come in the following standard sizes: From 3/16" to 9/16" by sixteenths; from 5/8" to 2" by eighths except 1⅛" and 1⅞"

Rectangular tool steel comes in the following standard sizes in thickness : From ⅛" to ⅜" by sixteenths; from ⅜" to 1" by eighths; and from 1" to 1½" by quarters. (In widths : From ½" to 6"

References:
Trade Catalogs.

CASE-HARDENING

Case-hardening consists essentially in converting the exterior or case of a piece of wrought-iron or soft steel into high-carbon tool steel without changing the character of the internal structure. The process consists in surrounding the pieces with some highly carbonaceous substance such as bone meal, charred leather scrap, or potassium cyanide and holding it to a high temperature for a period of time. The thickness of the coat required will determine the length of time the pieces must be left in the compound. Pieces are usually left in bone meal for several hours or even days. In potassium cyanide, however, the required thickness may be obtained in from thirty minutes to an hour and one-half. The metal absorbs carbon from the material surrounding it thus converting it into high carbon steel. After case-hardening, the surface has all of the characteristics of tool steel and may be plunged and hardened.

By case-hardening we get a product that has a hard wear-resisting surface or case combined with a tough soft steel center. This is often highly desirable in manufacturing certain parts for machines. The wrist pin in a gas engine will illustrate the point. A wrist pin must have a wear-resisting outer shell, but it need not be hard all the way thru. In fact, if the pin were hardened all the way thru it would be highly susceptible to crystallization. A case-hardened, soft-steel pin is very resilient and will absorb the shock or force of the explosion without the danger of crystallization.

Potassium cyanide is generally used for case-hardening. It is a highly poisonous chemical and must be handled with great care. It should not be allowed to come in contact with scratches or open wounds, nor should the fumes be inhaled.

References:

Bacon, *Forge Practice*, p. 232. Harcourt, *Elementary Forge Practice*, p. 112.

TAPS AND DIES

There are two types of threads in general use.

(1) The U. S. S. (United States Standard) is in common use in machinery and for most other purposes except where the thread is in soft metal.

2) The S. A. E. Society of Automotive Engineers) has a finer pitch to the thread and is used where fine adjustments and great security is needed. It is the standard thread used in automobile construction.

A complete set of taps consists of three taps for each size:

(1 The *taper tap*, which is tapered to a long taper so that the end is smaller than the drill hole in which the threads are to be cut. This makes it easy to start the tap properly. The taper tap is generally used where the hole goes thru the stock and no other tap is necessary.

2) The *plug tap* is only slightly tapered and is used to start the thread in blind holes.

3) The *bottoming tap* is used to follow the plug tap to cut a thread to the bottom of a blind hole.

Dies are either solid or adjustable. The solid dies usually are made 1/32" oversize for rough work. The adjustable die may be adjusted to cut over or under. It should never be used without first examining it to see that it is properly adjusted.

Taps and dies are easily damaged by careless handling. They should be kept oiled with a light oil and kept in a box where they will not come in contact with other tools or with each other.

References:

Jones, *Forging and Smithing*, p. 34.

EXPANSION OF IRON AND STEEL

When iron and steel are heated they expand, when cooled they contract. When work is being done that requires great accuracy the expansion of the metal must be taken into consideration. Expansion is made use of in doing such work as shrinking tires, shrinking bands, etc. The rate of expansion is uniform as the temperature rises. The expansion of a piece of iron or steel when the temperature is raised from room temperature to a cherry red heat is approximately one-tenth of an inch per foot. When heated to a bright red heat the expansion is approximately one-eighth inch per foot. By means of these figures the amount of the expansion of a tire or band may be readily calculated by first finding the length of the tire or band in feet and then multiplying by the amount of expansion per foot.

FILES

There are three classes of files; namely, rasp cut, single-cut and double-cut. Under each of the above classes we have four grades or degrees of coarseness; namely, coarse, bastard, second-cut, and smooth. There are many shapes of files, but the most common shapes are rectangular or flat, triangular or three-cornered, half round, round or rat tail, and square. The ordinary flat file is used by the blacksmith for all general purposes, but such jobs as saw sharpening require a special kind of file. Sometimes a flat file is provided with one smooth edge or safe edge so that the filing may be done in a corner without cutting the side of the corner

References:
Nicholson, *File Filosophy*.

EMERY WHEEL TEST FOR DETERMINING KINDS OF MATERIALS

The most common method of differentiating between the different grades of tool steel, soft steel and iron is the emery wheel test. It consists in placing the stock against the emery wheel and observing the shower of sparks that come off the wheel while the stock is being ground. Each kind of material will give off sparks distinctly different in appearance. High-carbon tool steel gives off a shower of very light red sparks which explode into many star-like shoots. As the percentage of carbon in the material decreases, the sparks become redder and the explosions into star-like particles are fewer Norway iron has a red spark with no star-like explosions.

The carbon content of material may be determined by comparing the sparks with the sparks of material with a known percentage of carbon. Files are known to contain a relatively high percentage of carbon, say about one-hundred point, and if touched to the emery wheel and ground, a light colored shower of sparks with numerous star-like explosions will come off the wheel. Since a file is always available it will be convenient to use this as a basis for comparison. If there are more star-like explosions the material being tested contains more carbon than the file. The more the shower tends toward a red non-explosive spark the smaller the percentage of carbon contained. In order to form a basis for judgment test several pieces by comparing the sparks with those of file.

References:

Harcourt, *Elementary Forge Practice*, p. 15.

STANDARD TABLES

TABLE NO. 1
Weights of Round and Square Iron and Steel Bars per Lineal Foot, in Pounds

Size In.	Round Iron	Round Steel	Square Iron	Square Steel	Size In.	Round Iron	Round Steel	Square Iron	Square Steel
¼	.164	.170	.208	.210	2½	16.36	16.68	20.83	21.20
5⁄16	.256	.260	.326	.330	2⅝	18.04	18.39	22.97	23.50
⅜	.368	.380	.469	.480	2¾	19.80	20.18	25.21	25.70
7⁄16	.501	.510	.638	.650	2⅞	21.64	22.06	27.55	28.20
½	.654	.670	.833	.850	3	23.56	24.10	30.00	30.60
9⁄16	.828	.850	1.055	1.080	3⅛	25.57	26.12	32.55	33.13
⅝	1.023	1.040	1.302	1.330	3¼	27.65	28.30	35.21	35.96
11⁄16	1.237	1.270	1.576	1.610	3⅜	29.82	30.45	37.97	38.64
¾	1.473	1.500	1.875	1.920	3½	32.07	32.70	40.83	41.60
13⁄16	1.728	1.760	2.201	2.240	3⅝	34.40	35.20	43.80	44.57
⅞	2.004	2.040	2.552	2.600	3¾	36.82	37.54	46.88	47.80
15⁄16	2.301	2.350	2.930	3.060	4	41.89	42.72	53.33	54.40
1	2.618	2.650	3.333	3.400	4¼	47.29	48.30	60.21	61.40
1⅛	3.313	3.380	4.219	4.300	4½	53.01	54.60	67.50	68.90
1¼	4.091	4.170	5.208	5.310	4¾	59.07	60.30	75.21	76.70
1⅜	4.950	5.050	6.302	6.430	5	65.45	66.80	83.33	85.00
1½	5.890	6.010	7.500	7.650	5¼	72.16	73.60	91.88	93.70
1⅝	6.913	7.050	8.802	8.980	5½	79.19	80.80	100.80	102.80
1¾	8.018	8.180	10.210	10.400	5¾	86.56	88.30	110.20	112.40
1⅞	9.204	9.380	11.720	11.900	6	94.25	96.10	120.00	122.40
2	10.470	10.710	13.330	13.600	6¼	102.30	104.30	130.20	132.80
2⅛	11.820	12.050	15.050	15.400	6½	110.60	112.80	140.80	143.60
2¼	13.250	13.600	16.880	17.200	7	128.30	130.90	163.30	166.60
2⅜	14.770	15.100	18.800	19.200		..	..	..	..

Weights of Flat Iron, per Lineal Foot, in Pounds

Width Inches	Thickness, Inches											
	⅛	3⁄16	¼	5⁄16	⅜	½	⅝	¾	1	1¼	1½	2
1	.42	.63	.83	1.04	1.25	1.67	2.08	2.50	3.33	4.17	5.00	6.67
1⅛	.47	.70	.94	1.17	1.41	1.87	2.34	2.81	3.75	4.69	5.63	7.50
1¼	.52	78	1.04	1.30	1.56	2.08	2.60	3.13	4.17	5.21	6.25	8.33
1⅜	.57	.86	1.15	1.43	1.72	2.29	2.86	3.44	4.58	5.73	6.88	9.17
1½	.63	.94	1.25	1.56	1.88	2.50	3.13	3.75	5.00	6.25	7.50	10.00
1⅝	.68	1.02	1.36	1.69	2.03	2.71	3.30	4.06	5.42	6.77	8.13	10.83
1¾	.73	1.09	1.46	1.82	2.19	2.92	3.65	4.38	5.83	7.29	8.75	11.67
2	.83	1.25	1.67	2.08	2.50	3.33	4.17	5.00	6.67	8.33	10.00	13.33
2¼	.94	1.41	1.88	2.34	2.81	3.75	4.65	5.63	7.50	9.38	11.25	15.00
2½	1.04	1.56	2.08	2.60	3.13	4.17	5.21	6.25	8.33	10.42	12.50	16.67
2¾	1.15	1.72	2.29	2.86	3.44	4.58	5.73	6.88	9.17	11.46	13.75	18.33
3	1.25	1.88	2.50	3.13	3.75	5.00	6.25	7.50	10.00	12.50	15.00	20.00
3¼	1.35	2.03	2.71	3.39	4.06	5.42	6.77	8.13	10.83	13.54	16.25	21.67
3½	1.46	2.19	2.92	3.65	4.38	5.83	7.29	8.75	11.67	14.58	17.50	23.33
3¾	1.56	2.34	3.13	3.91	4.69	6.25	7.81	9.38	12.50	15.63	18.75	25.00
4	1.67	2.50	3.33	4.17	5.00	6.67	8.33	10.00	13.33	16.67	20.00	26.67
4½	1.88	2.81	3.75	4.69	5.63	7.50	9.38	11.25	15.00	18.75	22.50	30.00
5	2.08	3.13	4.17	5.21	6.25	8.33	10.42	12.50	16.07	20.83	25.00	33.33
5½	2.29	3.44	4.58	5.73	6.88	9.17	11.46	13.75	18.33	22.92	27.50	36.67
6	2.50	3.75	5.00	6.25	7.50	10.00	12.50	15.00	20.00	25.00	30.00	40.00
7	2.92	4.38	5.83	7.29	8.75	11.67	14.58	17.50	23.33	29.17	35.00	46.67
8	3.33	5.00	6.67	8.32	10.00	13.33	16.67	20.00	26.67	33.32	40.00	53.33

TABLE NO. 2. OCTAGON BARS

Size inches	Pounds per foot	Size inches	Pounds per foot	Size inches	Pounds per foot
¼	0.1760				
9/32	0.2228	29/32	2.3133	1 17/32	6.604
5/16	0.2751	15/16	2.4756	1 9/16	6.877
11/32	0.3328	31/32	2.6434	1 19/32	7.154
⅜	0.3961	1	2.8167	1 ⅝	7.438
13/32	0.4649	1 1/32	2.995	1 21/32	7.727
7/16	0.5391	1 1/16	3.180	1 11/16	8.021
15/32	0.6189	1 3/32	3.370	1 23/32	8.321
½	0.7042	1 ⅛	3.565	1 ¾	8.626
17/32	0.7949	1 5/32	3.766	1 25/32	8.937
9/16	0.8912	1 3/16	3.972	1 13/16	9.253
19/32	0.9930	1 7/32	4.184	1 27/32	9.575
⅝	1.1003	1 ¼	4.401	1 ⅞	9.902
21/32	1.2130	1 9/32	4.624	1 29/32	10.235
11/16	1.3313	1 5/16	4.852	1 15/16	10.573
23/32	1.4551	1 11/32	5.086	1 31/32	10.917
¾	1.5844	1 ⅜	5.325	2	11.267
25/32	1.7191	1 13/32	5.570		
13/16	1.8594	1 7/16	5.820		
27/32	2.0052	1 15/32	6.076		
⅞	2.1565	1 ½	6.337		

The size of octagon bars is the distance between opposite faces.

TABLE NO. 3. WIRE GAGE STANDARDS IN USE IN THE UNITED STATES

DIMENSIONS OF SIZES ARE IN DECIMAL PARTS OF AN INCH

Number of wire gage	American or Brown & Sharpe	Birmingham or Stubbs' iron wire	Washburn & Moen	W & M. steel music wire	New American S. & W. Co.'s music wire	Imperial wire gage	Stubbs' steel wire	U. S. standard gage for sheet & plate iron & steel	Number of wire gage
00	.365	.380	.331	.013	.008	.348		.344	00
0	.325	.340	.306	.014	.009	.324	..	.312	0
1	.289	.300	.283	.015	.010	.300	.227	.281	1
2	.258	.284	.262	.017	.011	.276	.219	.266	2
3	.229	.259	.244	.018	.012	.252	.212	.250	3
4	.204	.238	.225	.019	.013	.232	.207	.234	4
5	.182	.220	.207	.020	.014	.212	.204	.219	5
6	.162	.203	.192	.021	.016	.192	.201	.203	6
7	.144	.180	.177	.023	.018	.176	.199	.187	7
8	.128	.165	.162	.024	.020	.160	.197	.172	8
9	.114	.148	.148	.026	.022	.144	.194	.156	9
10	.102	.134	.135	.027	.024	.128	.191	.141	10
11	.091	.120	.120	.028	.026	.116	.188	.125	11
12	.081	.109	.105	.030	.029	.104	.185	.109	12
13	.072	.095	.091	.031	.031	.092	.182	.094	13
14	.064	.083	.080	.033	.033	.080	.180	.078	14
15	.057	.072	.072	.034	.035	.072	.178	.070	15
16	.051	.065	.062	.036	.037	.064	.175	.062	16
17	.045	.058	.054	.038	.039	.056	.172	.056	17
18	.040	.049	.048	.039	.041	.048	.168	.050	18
19	.036	.042	.041	.041	.043	.040	.164	.044	19
20	.032	.035	.035	.043	.045	.036	.161	.037	20
21	.028	.032	.032	.046	.047	.032	.157	.034	21
22	.025	.028	.029	.048	.049	.028	.155	.031	22
23	.023	.025	.026	.051	.051	.024	.153	.028	23
24	.020	.022	.023	.055	.055	.022	.151	.025	24
25	.018	.020	.020	.059	.059	.020	.148	.022	25
26	.016	.018	.018	.063	.063	.018	.146	.019	26
27	.014	.016	.017	.066	.067	.016	.143	.017	27
28	.013	.014	.016	.072	.071	.015	.139	.016	28
29	.011	.013	.015	.076	.075	.014	.134	.014	29
30	.010	.012	.014	.080	.080	.012	.127	.012	30

TABLE NO. 4. BOLTS AND CAP SCREWS

United States Standard			S.A.E.			Machine Screws			Pipe Threads		
Size	Threads per inch	Tap drill	Size	Threads per inch	Tap drill	Size	Threads per inch	Tap drill	Nominal size	Threads per inch	Tap drill
1/4	20	3/16	1/4	28	7/32	2	48	50	1/8	27	11/32
5/16	18	17/64	5/16	24	17/64	2	56	49	1/4	18	21/32
3/8	16	21/64	3/8	24	21/64	3	48	45	3/8	18	19/32
7/16	14	3/8	7/16	20	3/8	3	56	44	1/2	14	23/32
1/2	13	13/32	1/2	20	7/16	4	48	44	3/4	14	15/16
9/16	12	29/64	9/16	18	1/2	4	36	48	1	11½	1 3/16
5/8	11	33/64	5/8	18	9/16	6	40	36	1¼	11½	1 15/32
11/16	11	37/64	11/16	16	39/64	6	32	40	1½	11½	1¾
3/4	10	5/8	3/4	16	43/64	8	36	30	2	11½	2 3/16
13/16	10	11/16	7/8	14	33/32	8	32	32			
7/8	9	47/64	1	14	29/32	10	32	25			
15/16	9	51/64				10	24	29			
1	8	27/32				12	28	18			
						12	24	20			
						14	24	12			
						14	20	16			
						18	20	1			
						18	18	2			

TABLE NO. 5. STOVE BOLTS

Size	Threads per inch	Tap drill size
1/8	32	44
5/32	28	35
3/16	25	29
7/32	22	20
1/4	18	3/16
5/16	18	1/4
3/8	16	11/32

TABLE NO. 6. COMMON STEEL WIRE NAILS

Size	Length inches	Wire gage	Number per pound
2d	1	15	876
3d	1¼	14	568
4d	1½	12½	316
5d	1¾	12½	271
6d	2	11½	181
7d	2¼	11½	161
8d	2½	10¼	106
9d	2¾	10¼	96
10d	3	9	69
12d	3¼	9	63
16d	3½	8	49
20d	4	6	31
30d	4½	5	24
40d	5	4	18
50d	5½	3	14
60d	6	2	11

TABLE NO. 7 DIAMETER OF WOOD SCREWS

Number	Diameter	Number	Diameter
0	.058	11	.203
1	.071	12	.216
2	.084	13	.229
3	.097	14	.242
4	.110	15	.255
5	.124	16	.268
6	.137	17	.282
7	.150	18	.295
8	.163	19	.308
9	.176	20	.321
10	.189		

Notes:

Notes:

www.ingramcontent.com/pod-product-compliance
Lightning Source LLC
Chambersburg PA
CBHW021109080526
44587CB00010B/446